BACH,
BEETHOVEN
AND THE BOYS

BACH, BEETHOVEN AND THE BOYS

Music History As It Ought To Be Taught

DAVID W. BARBER

SOUND AND VISION
TORONTO

TABLE OF CONTENTS

AUTHOR'S NOTE & ACKNOWLEDGEMENTS

WHEN I WAS STUDYING MUSIC at Queen's University (believe it or not, I did earn an honors B.Mus. degree, with a concentration in voice performance and music history), one of my music-history professors gently pulled me aside one day and told me that, although my work was good, I was "too easily distracted by the non-essentials." This book will, I suppose, only confirm that judgment.

I feel it's important to stress that the historical information in this book is all true (well, *almost* all of it is true). When Bach left Cöthen for Leipzig, he really *did* have 11 linen shirts "at the wash." If you don't believe me you could look it up for yourself.

Some well-meaning former friends of mine who read the manuscript in preparation made the comment that they found all the footnotes distracting. If you have this problem, too, please feel free to ignore the footnotes. But I warn you, you'd be missing some of the best parts.[1]

Thanks to the usual round of friends and relations for moral support and patiently enduring my *historicomical* ramblings and *non sequiturs*, and to Geoff and Jacky Savage of Sound And Vision and Dave Donald for his illustrations and expertise.

I'm glad for this 10th-anniversary edition, which offers the chance to correct many niggling errors — without (I hope) introducing any new ones.

DWB
Kingston, 1986; Toronto, 1996

---

[1]Alternatively, you could read only the footnotes and ignore the main body of the text. Suit yourself.

III

ABOUT THE AUTHOR

David Barber is a journalist and musician and the author of five other humorous books about music. Formerly the entertainment editor of the Kingston *Whig-Standard*, he now divides his time between working as a copyeditor at the Toronto *Globe and Mail* and, with his wife, Judy Scott, operating their bookstore/café, White Knight Books and The Dormouse Café, in Westport, Ont. As a composer, his works include two symphonies, a jazz mass based on the music of Dave Brubeck, a *Requiem*, several short choral works and numerous vocal-jazz arrangements. In his spare time he is an avid kayaker and reader of mysteries and enjoys performing with his vocal-jazz group, Barber and the Sevilles.

ABOUT THE ILLUSTRATOR

Dave Donald can't remember when he didn't scrawl his little marks on most surfaces, so it doesn't come as much of a surprise that he now makes a living doing just that. He is currently freelancing his way through life and doing all the things he wanted to do if he didn't have a full-time job. Dave is an avid music listener who likes to look for the funny side in anything. Classical music gives him lots to look at. This book represents his second illustrative collaboration with David Barber.

PREFACE

IT WAS HIGH TIME SOMEBODY did for the history of
music what Messrs Sellar and Yeatman did for the history
of England. Those of you learned enough to know *1066 And
All That* will remember that Julius Caesar came to Britain and
found the woad-painted inhabitants "weeny, weedy and weaky"
and that the Romans were Top Nation at the time because of
their classical education. Anglo-Saxon England had kings with
names like Filthfroth and Brothelbreath. William-and-Mary
were stuck together like copulating dogs, and so on. And all
that. Without the benefit of a collaborator, David W. Barber has
ranged a bigger world than England and come up with a work
funnier than that classic misguide to historical truth. He has
done the job, and nobody else has to do it now.

The point I want to make now before you meet B. and B.
(to say nothing of the B. named Johannes and for that matter,
the one called Benjamin or Bela) is that what you will be laughing at is the truth. There is not a single false note in this short-
playing record. If Barber says that Richard Wagner was born in
1813, you can take it that he was. Check in Grove's twenty-vol-
ume *Dictionary of Music and Musicians* if you like, but the
effort, to say nothing of the money, won't procure you a more
accurate date. If he says that Stravinsky's *Rite of Spring* was first
performed in Paris in 1913, there is no need for you to consult
my father, who swore he was there. You can't consult him, anyway, for he has joined the great democracy of the dead wherein
cinema pianists (my father was one of those) lie snugly with vir-
tuosi, John Lennon and academic stretto-wanglers. Barber,
however, tells us something you won't find in Grove — name-
ly, that Nijinsky made an erotic gesture during the performance
and this did not please the Parisians, who knew all about erotic

gestures but, with Gallic *savoir-faire*, liked to keep them in their place or places, one of which was not the opera house.

That Barber was the one man for this sane and demented history should have been apparent to all who consulted *A Musician's Dictionary*, which contains such wisdom as "English Horn: A woodwind instrument so named because it is neither English nor a horn. Not to be confused with the French Horn, which is German" and "Wrong Notes: it must be understood that this is a relative term, and applies only to those examples performed by someone else. Wrong notes performed by oneself are always referred to as ornaments." The Barber history, which is ready to explode on you as soon as you have read, if you have, I don't care much anyway, this preface, is equally wise, meaning mad. With music the two terms do not square up to each other in anything like a meaningful opposition. Wise men look like Beethoven, meaning they didn't wash and have lost their hair brush, and Beethoven was certainly mad. I mean, you have to be mad to practise an art that doesn't know why it exists in the first place. I mean, we know what hamburgers are for, also sex, but we don't know the purpose of music. That's why we have Muzak, which knows all too well why it exists. It exists primarily because nobody knows how to switch it off.

By a curious chance (I do not joke, any more than Barber does) I got up at five this morning because my cough was keeping my sleeping partner awake (my wife, if you must know). As any musician will tell you, there is only one thing to do when you wake at five, and that is to compose a fugue. I composed a fugue, and then the mail came, with Barber's typescript. It is a fugue for four voices, in A minor. It is the twenty-second fugue I have written in little over a week. God knows why I am writing fugues. It is certainly not to awaken the sleeping soul of Bach. Fugue is something that gets into you and, when one has composed forty-eight of the bastards, flies, or fugues, out again. Barber's book confirmed that I am not alone in my madness. It made me feel better, and it cured my cough.

No, it (damn and blast it) didn't.

So my heartiest commendation of an admirable work of scholarship — "gapped," true, as academics say of melodies that are, in fact, gapped but, where there are no gaps, crammed with accuracy. I will not say again that it is funny, since this will compel you to set your jaw and dare Barber to make you laugh. Take it for its truth. When you have read it you will know a great deal of musical history. Whether you will think it worth knowing is another matter. For music is another name for dementia. Who would spend his life spinning combinations of twelve notes if he were sane? There are better things worth spinning, but I can't think just what they are at the moment. I got up too early.

© Anthony Burgess
Monte Carlo, December 7, 1985

GETTING THE BALL ROLLING

EARLY MUSIC

ALTHOUGH THE ANCIENT GREEKS had a thing or two to say about music,[1] and before that prehistoric Man probably hummed some sort of mastodon-hunting song as he set off from his cave each morning, music history as we know it is usually said to have begun with Gregorian chant, on the theory that it had to start *somewhere*.

... some sort of mastodon-hunting song ...

It came about like this: one morning, back in the sixth century or so, a bunch of the boys at the local monastery got together for a regular morning of worship. One of the monks had been up to late the night before, translating a passage of Paul's letter to the Ephesians or some such, and fell asleep in the middle of the service. In order to hide from the abbot the sound of his snoring, some of the other monks began to sing verses of the daily psalm. Chanting was born.

Actually, there is no evidence whatsoever to support this

---

[1] Plato thought it was a pretty good idea, though with some reservations.

theory. But it makes at least as much sense as what Pope Gregory told everyone: he said a dove had flown down from heaven, perched on his shoulder, and dictated all the chants into his ear. Take your pick.

At any rate, by about the ninth century the principles of Gregorian chant were established as a sort of monastic etiquette, telling the monks what to sing and when and for how long. Guido of Arezzo was the one who figured out that the scribes would have any easier time writing down the music if they had the lines to guide them.[2] If he'd thought harder, he might have gone to fame and fortune by inventing the coloring book.

Guido was a clever fellow but he had a low opinion of singers. He said they were "the most stupid men of our times."[3] He also had some nasty things to say about monks. He thought they spent too much time trying to sing and not enough time studying the Scriptures. He was always complaining about something. Guido is most famous for inventing the Guidonian Hand, which is a funny little drawing of a hand with squiggles all over it. He claimed that by studying the little squiggles you could remember all the notes of every plainchant mode.[4] Nowadays, hardcore musicians put posters of Guido's hand on their walls to make themselves look scholarly.

Monks divided the day into successive Hours, which they also called Offices. (Each monk had a little sign on the door to his room that said "Office Hours.") Each office had its own particular music that would be sung every day. This was strictly codified. When it came to singing, the Gregorians left nothing to chance.

Plainsong was sung in three different styles, depending on how many notes there were in each syllable of the text. If there was only one note it was called syllabic; with two or three notes, neumatic.[5] If there were so many notes that you forgot what word you were singing, that was melismatic.

Eventually, some of the melismatic sections got so convoluted that someone had the idea of putting words back into them again. Often it had been so long since anyone had sung the words that no one could remember what they had been singing

[2] Before that it was rather haphazard.
[3] It sounds more polite in Latin: "*Temporibus nostris super omnes homines fatui sunt cantores.*" But it isn't.
[4] Don't panic: modes are really just like scales.
[5] Or pneumatic, since it took more air.

4

about in the first place so the new words had little to do with the original text. These new texts were known as tropes and they were rather entertaining until some spoilsport on the Council of Trent banned them all in the 16th century.

For people who are more familiar with later styles of music, Gregorian chant takes some getting used to. The sound of men's voices on a single line sounds more like a swarm of bees. But it's really very beautiful if you give it a chance.[6]

There were hardly any women involved in all of this. It was mostly men. If you're looking for someone to blame, blame St. Paul. In his first epistle to the Corinthians he says *"Mulieres in ecclesiis taceant,"* or "Let your women keep silence in the churches." Everyone took him literally.

Anonymous IV

Gregorian chants developed into something called *organum*, which was all the rage of the ninth to 12th centuries. In its simplest form, this consisted of singing the same Gregorian tune as the monk beside you at an interval of a perfect fourth or fifth.[7] This is harder to do than it sounds, and requires the kind of concentration that monks are especially good at.

Sophisticated *organum* was developed into a high art form by two composers at the Cathedral of Notre Dame in Paris in the 12th and 13th centuries: Leonin and his successor, Perotin. They published a collection of their music in a big book called *Magnus Liber*.[8]

Much of what we know about the music of Leonin and Perotin comes to us from a treatise by anonymous Englishman, written about 1280. He differs from almost all other anonymous writers because he has a name. Well, sort of. To distin-

[6] Useful too. The time it takes to chant the *Miserere* (Psalm 51) is just right for steeping a pot of tea.

[7] It's not worth explaining why fourths and fifths are called perfect. Just take my word for it.

[8] Which is Latin for "Big Book."

guish him from all the other anonymous writers, he is referred to as Anonymous IV.[9] Of all the Anonymouses through all the years, Anonymous IV is the only one anyone remembers by name. His mother must be very proud, whoever she is.

One of the most important features of the Notre Dame motet is its use of rhythmic patterns, or modes.[10] Whole academic careers have been based on finding whether Perotin meant the tunes to go "*dum*-ti-*dum*" or "ti-*dum*-ti-*dum.*" For some people, this is an earth-shattering decision. Two French musicologists, named Beck and Aubry, went so far as to fight a sword duel over the issue in 1910. Musicology hasn't seen anything quite as exciting since.[11]

A troubador.   *A trouvere.*

Meanwhile, as all this church music was going on, the troubadours and trouveres were busy singing racier songs about true love and good wine. And how much better one was with the other.

It is nearly impossible to distinguish between troubadours and trouveres. And don't let anyone con you into believing oth-

[9]Anonymouses I to III never amounted to much.
[10]Pay attention: these aren't the same as the old Gregorian modes.
[11]Aubry lost. He died of embarrassment, or stab wounds, or both.

erwise. Troubadours tended to hang around the south of France and travel north. Trouveres hung around the north and went south. Other than that, they're pretty much the same.

The most important thing to remember if you were a troubadour [12] was to sing a heartfelt song about how much you loved the woman of your dreams: how lovely her hair was, how beautiful her eyes and skin, how much you longed to kiss her — that sort of thing. You and the object of your love were meant for each other. True love like this had never before been seen. If only you could rid of the husband, everything would be perfect. [13]

By the 14th century, this tradition of songs about unrequited love had developed into a real industry, almost as big as the pop songs of today. Everybody composed weepy songs about lost loves and cruel beauties. In between sobbing fits they managed to write some of the music down into fancy heart-shaped manuscripts. [14] The 20th-century descendants of these composers grew up to become copywriters for the major greeting-card companies.

---

[12] Or trouvere.
[13] There's always a catch.
[14] They thought it looked cute.

NOW WE'RE GETTING SOMEWHERE

JOSQUIN

JOSQUIN DES PREZ, ONE HISTORIAN tells us, "emerges from the mists" in the 1460s or '70s in Milan. He had to come out of the fog to see what he was writing.

Josquin was born about 1440 in Picardy and probably studied music under the composer Okeghem. Okeghem was a big noise in his own time but today we pay more attention to Josquin.[1]

Other than that, we don't know a whole lot about Josquin's life. He travelled a lot, working as a singer and composer for popes, kings and other bigshots in Milan and Rome, and also at the court of the French king, Louis XII.

Josquin had a reputation for being a bit headstrong — one of those brilliant but moody types. When the Duke of Ferrara was considering hiring Josquin as court composer, the duke's secretary recommended that he hire Isaac instead. Isaac, the secretary said, got along better with people and composed music more quickly. Not better, but faster. Besides, Josquin wanted 200 ducats and Isaac would do the job for only 120. Josquin got the job anyway. That's the great thing about being a duke: you can ask for advice and then ignore it.

Josquin also had a wicked sense of humor. After he grew tired of waiting for a raise the French king had promised him, Josquin composed a motet on the text, "Remember thy word unto thy servant." Louis got the message and Josquin got his money, whereupon he composed another motet, "Lord, thou has dealt graciously with thy servant."[2] For Josquin, composing motets was the Renaissance equivalent of writing interoffice memos.

Josquin seemed to have an obsession with money.[3] One of

---

[1] That's the way it goes
[2] Subtle, wasn't he?
[3] It comes with the job. The obsession, not the money.

his best chansons is *Faulte d'argent*, which is all about what a bore it is to have no money. "If I say so," Josquin's text says, "it is because I know."

A popular composing technique in those days was to build a mass or motet around the melody of a *cantus firmus*, or "fixed song."[4] The *cantus firmus* (C.F. to its friends) was taken from Gregorian chant or from some other well-known song of the day. Try to imagine an entire mass based on the tune of *Home On The Range* and you'll get the idea. Among the best-known C.F. melodies is one called *L'Homme armé*, all about a man with a sword in his hand.[5]

The Renaissance equivalent of writing interoffice memos.

In Josquin's day you were nobody unless you had composed at least one *L'Homme armé* mass. Josquin composed two, just to be on the safe side.

Josquin eventually grew tired of life on the road and returned to his Picardy home in his final years. He died in 1521, leaving the way clear for those composers known as the "post-Josquin generation." These included Nicholas Gombert, Adrian Willaert and Clemens non Papa. The reason for this last man's unusual nickname is not fully understood. But it probably had nothing to do with a paternity suit.

[4] This implies that at some point the song must have been broken
[5] If you listen closely, you'll hear that it sounds a lot like the Beatles' song *Sgt. Pepper's Lonely Hearts Club Band*. Really.

PALESTRINA

IT MIGHT CONFUSE YOU TO learn that Palestrina is not a person but a place. The composer was actually named Giovanni Pierluigi da Palestrina. At various times he was also known as Joannes Petrus-Aloysius Praenestinus, Joannes Praenestinus, Giovanni da Penestrina, Geo Pietro Luigi da Pallestrina, Gianetti Palestina, Gianetto del Palestino, Gio Petralosis Prenestrino and Gianetto Palestrina. Under the circumstances, Palestrina seems the least trouble.

He was born around 1525 to Santo and his wife Palme Pierluigi, in a little house on the Via Cecconi in the tiny village of Palestrina, outside Rome. When his paternal grandmother died she left him a mattress and some kitchen utensils. But since he was only two years old at the time they wouldn't have been much use to him.

Gianetto (as he was called then) was a happy, playful child who became an altar boy and sang in the local choir. When he was twelve he went to Rome to a choir school, where he was taught elementary composition and how to make spitballs. When he was 20 he got his first job as an organist back in his home town. He married a girl named Lucrezia Gori, whose father had just died and left her some money.[1] At last he found a use for that mattress from his grandmother.

Not long after, Giovanni Maria del Monte, the bishop of Palestrina, became Pope Julius III and moved to Rome. Julius showed his appreciation of local talent by appointing Palestrina director of St Peter's choir.[2] For this he was paid six *scudi* every month. This would mean more if we knew how much a *scudo*

---

[1] The happy couple also inherited a house, a vineyard, some meadows and a chestnut-colored donkey.

[2] It just goes to show you should always be nice to people, just in case.

13

was worth, but we don't.[3] Palestrina was later made a singer in that pontifical choir, even though he didn't have a very good voice.[4] His pay went up to ten *scudi* a month.[5]

Julius III died in 1555 and was replaced by Pope Marcellus II, who reigned for a grand total of three weeks. He died suddenly when something he ate didn't agree with him.[6] Marcellus II would hardly be worth mentioning except that Palestrina dedicated his *Missa Papae Marcelli* to him, thereby single-handedly saving the future of music forever. Well, that's what his biographer Giuseppe Baini says, and who are we to disagree with him?

It seems that church music at the time had gotten a little too racy and the new pope, Paul IV, called for it to be cleaned up. Composers had been using bawdy songs as the basis for their church music. Worst of all, no one could understand the words.

The story goes that some of the stuffier cardinals wanted to abolish polyphony altogether and get back to the basics with Gregorian chant. Palestrina showed them the *Pope Marcellus Mass* and was able to convince them that some of this music could be quite respectable. Evidently the cardinals fell for it.

Palestrina was by no means your typical artsy-fartsy musician. He was a pretty shrewd businessman who sold barrels of sacramental wine to the church to make extra money. He wasn't very good at saving, though. When his son Angelo died suddenly, Palestrina had to borrow money to repay the bride's dowry, which he'd spent already.

Palestrina's wife died in 1580 of the dreaded sheep flu, which left the composer quite upset. For a while he even considered giving up music and becoming a priest. He got as far as shaving his head and then changed his mind. He married Virginia Dormuli, a rich widow, and took over her dead husband's fur and leather business, which had a monopoly to supply ermine trim to the Papal court. Fortunately, he hadn't yet taken a vow of celibacy.

Palestrina went into partnership with the shop's young apprentice and together they made a killing in the market.

[3] It was about equal to one medieval crown, if that's any help.
[4] It was mediocre, even for a tenor.
[5] He wasn't always paid in *scudi*. He once led the choir at another church and was given two goats.
[6] And don't call it poison. That's not polite.

Palestrina's wife was no fool, either. She invested 500 *scudi* into the business, which she later withdrew and lent back to Palestrina at eight-per-cent interest. He owned four houses, which he rented out to quiet tenants.

In the mornings Palestrina unplugged his tenants' toilets

Palestrina was very busy. In the mornings he minded the fur store and unplugged his tenants' toilets; in the afternoons he composed motets and masses. Somehow he found time to write 93 masses and 500 motets, not to mention the four books of madrigals and other assorted church music.[7]

But this output is nothing compared to the vast number of works — nearly 2,000 — composed by Palestrina's contemporary, Orlando di Lasso.[8] He was born in Belgium in 1530 or so and had such a fine voice as a boy that he was kidnapped three times by rival choirs.

Lasso did very well for himself, always managing to get hired by rich patrons who let him travel all over Europe in grand style. Once when the church authorities organized a solemn proces-

[7] The madrigals were a bit embarrassing, since everyone expected him to be the champion of pure church music. He later said "I blush and grieve" to admit that he had written them. Well, he was only young.

[8] Or Roland de Lassus, or — oh, let's not go through that again.

sion through the streets of Munich the parade was nearly ruined when it looked like it was going to rain. As soon as the choir began to sing Lasso's music, the clouds parted and the sun shone. Thereafter, the same piece was sung at all outdoor processions, just to be on the safe side.

Lasso enjoyed tremendous popularity as a composer and had his music performed in all the best places.[9] Although he was quite wild as a young man, he got more serious as he grew older. Pretty soon he'd stopped writing dirty songs altogether. Towards the end he went a bit bonkers. He no longer recognized his wife and had started to mumble.

For all-round piety it's hard to beat Tomas Luis de Victoria, who was a Spanish composer of the same period. He was also a priest. He kept saying that he was going to give up composing and devote himself to contemplating higher things. But somehow he never quite got around to it.[10]

Victoria studied in Rome before returning to Spain and admired Palestrina so much that he even took to copying his style of clothing and the way he trimmed his beard.

Victoria wasn't the only one who admired Palestrina, who even in his own time was better respected than most musicians ever manage today. Just two years before Palestrina's death, a group of other composers got together and printed some music, which they dedicated to Palestrina, whom they called: "an ocean of musical knowledge." They said that compared to him they were merely "rivers whose life is bound up with the sea." Palestrina was flattered, but had to ask them to stop before his feet got too wet.

Palestrina died in 1594 and was buried in the St. Peter's cemetery. Over the years, what with all the renovations and everything, we seem to have misplaced his grave. But he's still there somewhere, decomposing.

[9]Charles Burney was probably just jealous when he said that compared to Palestrina Lasso was "a dwarf on stilts."
[10]Maybe there *are* no higher things.

GESUALDO

IN THE GENERAL SCHEME OF MUSIC history, Don Carlo Gesualdo is not a terribly important figure. On the other hand, he is remarkable for two reasons: he is the only famous musician to be a true-born member of the nobility, and he is the only one (that we know of) ever to have murdered his wife. A few other musicians have been murdered.[1] But Gesualdo is the only one to have been a murderer himself. Besides, his music is strange. Even the right notes sound funny. Wrong ones are awful.

Gesualdo was born in 1560 into a family of the Italian nobility. He was Prince of Venosa, Count of Consa, Lord of Gesualdo, Marquis of Laino and a whole bunch of other high-sounding things besides.[2] His family tree went back all the way to before Charlemagne. His ancestors had a habit of either fighting a lot in wars or becoming bishops. They didn't believe in the middle ground.

Gesualdo grew up in very comfortable surroundings. There was nothing he liked better as a young man than to get together with a bunch of his friends, go away to the family castle outside Naples and sing madrigals all night. It disturbed the neighbors, but since he was a prince they couldn't complain.

The party ended for Gesualdo in 1585. His older brother Luigi died, leaving Gesualdo heir to the family name. This meant getting married — something he wasn't keen to do.[3] Gesualdo married his cousin Donna Maria d'Avalos, who at the age of 25 had married twice before already. That should have told him something.

---

[1] Not as many as there should have been, some might say.
[2] Although his wife called him something else entirely.
[3] Being a bachelor was more fun.

The wedding celebration was a big bash that lasted for days. Everyone drank too much and Gesualdo and his buddies sang off-key well into the small hours.

The marriage went along all right for a few years. Well enough for the couple to have a baby boy, anyway. But pretty soon Donna Maria began to resent the fact that Gesualdo was more interested in composing madrigals than in her. She began spending time with a certain Fabrizio Carafa, who was a duke and a count and rather dashing.

After that, they found excuses to be together most of the time, and pretty soon people were beginning to talk.[4] Word of the affair eventually got to Gesualdo, who changed all the locks on the palace doors. This only worked for a while. Donna Maria had new keys made, which she gave to Carafa.

Finally, one day in October, Gesualdo told his wife he was going out hunting and made a big show of riding off to the country. He had told her not to expect him home that night. She knew a good chance when she saw one and invited Carafa to come over. She said she needed a big, strong man to open jam jars or something

That night, Gesualdo returned secretly to the palace and caught his wife in bed with her lover.[5] He shot them both and then stabbed them a few times for good measure. Historian Cecil Gray agrees with the English essayist Thomas de Quincey that murder should be considered an art form. Gray gives Gesualdo points for the pistols and swordplay, but says he should have hit her a few times with a club. "A few judicious blows with a bludgeon," he says, "impart a variety, expressiveness and rich charm."[6]

After the murder, Gesualdo worried that people might be angry at him — his wife's family, for instance — so he escaped to his family castle and cut down all the trees so no one could sneak up on him. Gesualdo had good cause for concern: the murdered duke had a nephew who had once hit a monk over the head and killed him, just for reciting a poem too loudly.

Not only did Gesualdo kill his wife and her lover, he also

---

[4] Carafa was lonely too. His wife was a religious fanatic and was inclined to shout in her sleep. It kept him awake.

[5] Carafa was wearing Donna Maria's nightgown at the time. It was white, with black lace collar and cuffs.

[6] I'm not making this up, you know.

killed their small baby. The boy was his wife's second child. Gesualdo noticed that the baby's face looked familiar, but it didn't look like him. In a fit of anger, Gesualdo put the baby in a cradle suspended on ropes from the ceiling and rocked it to death.[7]

Carafa was wearing Donna Maria's nightgown at the time.

Needless to say, the murders were cause for much gossip. All the poets wrote about the event, but they tended to side with Gesualdo's wife, not him. They said he over-reacted.

Gesualdo married again a few years later. His second wife was Donna Eleonora d'Este, and she outlived him. But their marriage wasn't exactly rosy. Gesualdo may not have known it, but she was probably having an affair with Cardinal Allesandro d'Este, who aside from being a man of the church was her half-brother. (Might as well get hung for a sheep as a lamb, she must have figured.)

After his second marriage, Gesualdo spent most of his time at the court of the Duke of Ferrara, who liked to have musicians and composers hanging around the place. Over the years, he'd had such famous composers as Josquin des Prez, Orlando di Lasso, Cipriano de Rore, Obrecht, Marenzio and others. Palestrina stayed there for a few years and even John Dowland dropped in once for a visit.

Gesualdo had published his first book of madrigals under the pseudonym of Gioseppe Pilonij, but now he began publish-

[7]Afterwards, he felt guilty about the whole thing and had a monastery built on the site. Then he felt better.

ing them under his own name. Maybe being an infamous murderer improved his sales.[8] Altogether, Gesualdo published six books of madrigals, almost all of them characterized by daring and unusual harmonic progressions.[9]

Maybe Gesualdo's peculiar harmonies had something to do with his chronic bowel troubles. According to one Don Ferrante della Marra, writing in 1632, Gesualdo was unable to defecate "unless ten or twelve men, whom he kept specially for the purpose, were to beat him violently three times a day, during which operation he was wont to smile joyfully." That probably explains everything.

[8] Gray points out that the bulk of his compositions came after the murders. He says music was a more satisfying creative outlet.
[9] Composer Igor Stravinsky called him "the crank of chromaticism."

A FEW ENGLISHMEN

BYRD
....

WILLIAM BYRD (1543-1623) was an Elizabethan and as such not only had difficulty with spelling, but also had a tendency to put Capitals in the Oddest of Places.[1] The capital of England, however, was still London, where Byrd spent a great deal of time.

Of Byrd's parents nothing is known, although it is reasonable to assume that he had the requisite number, one of each. He spent his childhood in Lincolnshire, where it is possible that his father was the original Lincolnshire Poacher.[2] Since Byrd was appointed organist to Lincoln Cathedral at the age of 20, we must assume that he had some previous musical training. Otherwise he couldn't have lasted as long as he did, which was about 10 years.[3]

After that, Byrd went to London and became a Gentleman of the Chapel Royal.[4] In addition, he and another composer, his teacher Thomas Tallis (sorry, but we really haven't time to talk more about him) were granted a monopoly on music publishing by Queen Elizabeth. This gave them exclusive right to print any music "either plaid or soonge," in any language whatsoever. Whether this right extended to include music that was striped or polka-dotted, as well as plaid, musicologists can only assume.

Not only were Tallis and Byrd the only ones allowed to print music, they were also the only ones allowed to print the ruled paper upon which music is composed. They had, in other

[1] Any spelling errors that occur within quotation marks are not the mistake of the present author, but are the result of diligent plagiarism.
[2] Not eggs: game.
[3] Or perhaps the entire congregation was tone deaf, which has been known to happen.
[4] Which was, in fact, the Royal Chapel.

words, cornered the market. Modern-day composers who are finding it difficult to have their work published would do well to keep this tactic in mind.

Elizabeth was fond of music: one biographer of her time said, "She sings quite exceptionally both with voice and hand." It must have been sign language.

It must have been sign language.

Some of the music Byrd wrote was intended to be performed at home, by people looking for something to do after dinner.[5] In the case of madrigals, each part was printed separately, or at clockwise angles on a single sheet, so that everyone could sit around a table and sing.[6] Since only the very clever host could be counted upon to always invite the right number of voice parts to a dinner party, the music was often designed to be suited to either "voyces or viols."[7] That way, any number of vocal lines could be played by a stringed instrument, although it was sometimes difficult to understand the words. If everyone played and no one sang, it became impossible.

Madrigal singing had become increasingly popular in England ever since the publication in 1588 of a set of madrigals, largely of Italian origin,[8] called *Musica Transalpina*. I take the time to mention this interesting fact only because no history of English Renaissance music would be complete without it, and it's likely to turn up on the exam.[9]

Most of Byrd's music was written to be performed in the context of a church service (for either church; Byrd wasn't choosy), so most of it is vocal music. Someone had come up with the devious observation that the more the choir sang, the less the clergy preached. This was considered to have been a good thing for everyone, except perhaps the clergy.[10]

Although Byrd is chiefly known for his sacred music, it ought to be remembered that he also wrote the entertaining little madrigal *Suzanna Fayre Sometime Assaulted Was By Two Old Men Desiring Of Her Cause*, which is about exactly what you think it is. By the time you've sung the title, it's half over. Even though one of the chief characteristics of a madrigal is its ability to use music to paint a clear picture of the words, this one is not, perhaps luckily, a very good example of that.

---

[5] Charades hadn't been invented yet. And even if there had been television there wouldn't have been anything worth watching except maybe a re-enactment of the Wars of the Roses, an early forerunner of the modern Rose Bowl.

[6] When they got tired of that, they could play bridge.

[7] Or sometimes "voices or vyols," or often vile voices.

[8] Written by large Italians. Or by Italians in large print.

[9] Hadn't I warned you there was going to be an exam?

[10] Byrd felt that singing was good for everyone, since it "doth open the pipes." He doesn't say which pipes.

CLARKE

JEREMIAH CLARKE (1670?-1707), whose dates are usually kept inside parentheses so they won't run away, was a near-contemporary of Henry Purcell.[1] He was the organist at St Paul's Cathedral in London and is best remembered as being the composer of Purcell's *Trumpet Voluntary*.[2] That is, he actually composed it, but many — thinking it was too good for him — attributed it to Purcell.

This seems unfair, even in the days before copyright and royalties.[3] This piece is also known as *The Prince Of Denmark's March*, but it is unlikely that the Prince of Denmark composed it.

Clarke had a disappointing love affair with one of the ladies in his parish. He was so upset he committed suicide. Unable to decide between drowning and hanging himself, he flipped a coin. It landed on its edge in the mud, so he went home and shot himself.

So he went home and shot himself.

---

[1] The little question mark means that no one is quite sure in what year he was born. His mother must remember, but no one has thought of asking her.
[2] Voluntary means that you don't have to play it if you don't want to.
[3] Though not before Royalty. They were all over the place.

PURCELL

HENRY PURCELL WAS PROBABLY born in 1659.[1] As with many other composers, especially early ones, Purcell's dates are uncertain. But one of them must have been fairly certain, at least: her name was Frances and she married him.

Purcell is generally considered to have been the greatest English composer since William Byrd (although nobody asked Byrd what he thought of all this). Fortunately for Henry, Byrd had been dead for several years when Purcell was born, so the two of them didn't have a showdown. (Also, Byrd — being dead — was less likely to take offence.)

It's a pity that we don't know when his birthday is, but the registrar of births can hardly be blamed. After all, how was he to know that this little boy was going to grow up to become one of England's greatest composers? He looked just like all the other little brats, crying and slobbering there in his diaper. Nowadays we keep more accurate records, just in case.[2]

Henry was the son of Thomas Purcell, and had an uncle named Henry, both of whom were also musicians. He also had a musician brother, Daniel.[3] It wasn't the first time in the history of music that there had been several members of the same family who were all musicians. By the time of J.S. Bach, the whole thing had gotten rather out of hand.

Purcell began his musical career as a boy, singing in the

---

[1] He was definitely born: it probably happened in 1659.

[2] Although there is no record of Purcell's birthday, there are lots of records of his music. Just look in the Schwann catalogue.

[3] Unless Thomas was his uncle, in which case Henry was his father. But no one ever thinks of calling him Henry Purcell II. He himself tried to keep the name alive by naming two of his sons Henry, but both of them died in infancy. You just can't win sometimes.

Chapel Royal.[4] The choristers of the Chapel Royal were led by Captain Cooke, who is not to be confused with *the* Captain Cook, who was someone else.[5]

Cooke (the musical one) had a difficult time of it, since the Restoration was just starting, and everything was in a mess. There hadn't been much music at all under Cromwell and everybody was a little out of practice. One writer goes so far as to tell us that there was "not one Lad ... capable of Singing his Part readily."[6] In order to ensure the best quality for the Chapel Royal, Cooke sent talent scouts all over the country to steal promising young boys from other choirs. The other choirs were not pleased, but the king thought it was wonderful.

After a few years of singing, Purcell was given the apprentice job of "keeper, maker, mender, repayrer and tuner of the regalls, organs, virginalls, flutes and recorders and all other kind of wind instruments whatsoever."[7] This was an impressive, if rather lengthy, job title. Purcell probably shortened it to something less cumbersome, such as "Maker of the King's Instruments," or just plain "Hank the Mender." Later he was appointed composer for the king's violins,[8] and still later was made organist at Westminster Abbey.

In 1682, Purcell was made a Gentleman of the Chapel Royal, where he sang alto and bass. It was very confusing for those around him. Just when they would get used to his alto voice he would belt out a low bass note. Extensive musicological research has proven that he probably didn't try to sing both parts at once. In addition to their regular salary, the Gentlemen were given an annual bonus. Originally this consisted of three deer, but was later changed to a sum of money, which was more easily divided among 32 men.[9]

---

[4] It was all right: he was a member of the choir. As such, he was entitled to wear a livery, which consisted of a "cloak of bastard scarlett cloth lyned with velvett." That probably doesn't mean what you think it does.

[5] Patrons who went to the Chapel expecting to hear salty yarns were sadly disappointed, as were those who went aboard Cook's ship *Endeavour* expecting to hear verse anthems.

[6] This was surely unfair. There must have been at least *one* — somewhere.

[7] He was given the job after his own voice broke. Perhaps they thought it qualified him.

[8] They didn't know how to compose themselves.

[9] It was certainly less messy.

Purcell was generally well paid for the various duties he performed for the king, which included composing music for coronations, weddings and birthdays,[10] and the comings and goings of Important Personages. (He was always being pestered to write Departing or Returning Odes. Sometimes he wished they'd just go away and leave him alone.)

He also composed odes to St. Cecilia, the patroness of music. He thought it might bring him luck, and he was right. Even though he was often paid out of Secret Service funds, that doesn't necessarily mean he was a spy.[11]

One historian has said that in the last few years of his life "music for the theatre continued to flow from Purcell's pen." We can picture him, seated at his desk, his pen overflowing, with pieces of blank manuscript paper scattered around to soak up the mess, hoping that at least some of it will be legible enough to be used in *Dioclesian* or *The Fairy Queen*.

Music for the theatre continued to flow from Purcell's pen

[10] There certainly has been a lot of talk about birthdays in this chapter, hasn't there?

[11] It's hard to imagine him with a pistol concealed in his ruffles, or hiding a coded message in one of his anthems.

In addition, as long as Queen Mary continued to have birthdays, Purcell was obliged to compose Birthday Odes for her.[12] Finally, she said she'd had enough, and died. To show her how grateful he was, Purcell wrote the *Funeral Music for Queen Mary*.[13]

This included several anthems, accompanied by "flat Mournfull Trumpets." Whether the trumpets were flat because they were mournful, or mournful because they were flat, we are not told. Perhaps they are lamenting the fact that they are not trumpets at all, but trombones (and no one likes to have his name wrong in the program).

At any rate, just to show that you can never be too sure that you aren't going to need some piece of music again, Purcell died the very next year. The same music was played at his own funeral, although no one ever thinks of calling it the *Funeral Music for Henry Purcell*.[14]

He died on November 21, 1695, the eve of St. Cecilia's Day. Some think Purcell was embarrassed that he hadn't completed an ode for that year, and dying was the only excuse he could think of.

Another legend about his death tells us that he came home late one night, after having a few drinks with the boys. His wife refused to let him in, whereupon he caught pneumonia and died. It's a great story, but it wasn't Purcell. It was Maurice Greene. Greene was a fine composer, but he has little enough to make him memorable, and it seems unfair to rob him of his one moment of glory.

We know it can't have been Purcell because intensive research has shown that November of that year had been particularly mild. That's the trouble with musicology: some smart-alec is always digging up weather reports and spoiling the fun.

[12] Perhaps he felt he ode it to her.
[13] Even though she wasn't in a position (lying down dead) to appreciate it fully.
[14] He wasn't really in any better condition than the queen to appreciate the music. But he'd already heard it.

GOING BAROQUE

MONTEVERDI

T HE RENAISSANCE ERA ENDED and the Baroque began on March 25th, 1600, at 4 o'clock in the afternoon. No other history of music has the courage to make this statement with such conviction. I just wanted to set the record straight and clear up any lingering misunderstanding. The Renaissance hung around for a few more decades in England, but on the European continent it was all washed up.[1]

Listeners had grown tired of hearing the same old polyphony of the so-called *ars perfecta* or "perfect art" to be found in the music of Josquin, Palestrina and the rest of that crowd. They wanted something new to listen to. And composers were willing to oblige, since they were running out of things to say in the old idiom anyway.

Claudio Monteverdi was one of the leading lights in the change from the old style to the new. He referred to the old polyphonic style as the "first practice." His newer style of music he called the "second practice." He told everybody that one of these days he would write a book explaining all about his views on this subject.[2]

Monteverdi was born in 1567 in Cremona, a little town in the north of Italy. Cremona was a pretty place to live: the houses were large and graceful, the streets wide and straight. But musically it was a bit of a bore, not nearly as exciting as Mantua or Ferrara or Venice. Monteverdi's father, like Handel's after him, was a barber-surgeon who later became a physician.

Monteverdi probably learned about music from singing in the Cremona cathedral. Church musicians were not as presti-

---

[1] The English were always a little behind the times. Trends sometimes took as long as 50 years to cross the English Channel.
[2] He never quite got around to it.

gious as musicians at the royal courts, but they were higher on the social ladder than the town minstrels, or *piffari*, whose job was to follow the mayor around and blow trumpets just before he said anything important or cut a ribbon or something.

Evidently Monteverdi learned well, because he published his first book of motets when he was only 15. They were written for only three voices, which is not so difficult as four voices, but was still something to be proud of. By the time he turned 20, Monteverdi had published five books of motets and madrigals in five years. These were written in the old-fashioned style. But he was just warming up. Obviously, Cremona was getting too small for his talents.

So, in 1591, Monteverdi packed a bag and set off for Mantua, where he became a composer at the court of Duke Vincenzo Gonzaga. Vincenzo's father, Guglielmo, had been a keen patron of the arts, and his court had attracted fine musicians and artists from across Europe.

Vincenzo wasn't half the man his father was, at least when it came to appreciating good music. He was a bit of a cad, in fact: a womanizer and a gambler. When he grew tired of his first wife, he divorced her on the grounds that she was "deformed." He didn't specify how. Her family countered that he was an impotent old so-and-so. Vincenzo then suggested a test of his virility with any virgin girl in Venice.[3] For some reason the matter was dropped.

Despite his character faults, Vincenzo did like music, if only as a means of impressing his mistresses. He once planned an elaborate spectacle with music, costumes, fancy tapestries and lots of good food, just to please his Spanish mistress Agnese d'Argotti. But everything was cancelled when she said she was bored with the idea. Monteverdi was kept busy composing for Vincenzo. There was a concert every Friday in the Great Hall of Mirrors. In 1592, Vincenzo took his army across the Alps to help Austria fight off the attacking Turks, and Monteverdi went along for the ride, although he didn't enjoy it very much. The fighting, however, impressed him so much that many years later he wrote a book of war-like madrigals.

Part of Monteverdi's annoyance came from having to pay

---

[3] Evidently the virgins of Mantua weren't good enough for him. Or maybe there weren't any left.

many of his travelling expenses out of his own pocket. Nowadays, that sort of expense would be considered a legitimate tax deduction.

Monteverdi went along for the ride.

In 1600, a music theorist named Giovanni Artusi published an attack on modern music, which he thought was totally incomprehensible. Artusi complained that new composers were breaking all the established rules, laid down after centuries of noble tradition.[4] Although he didn't name Monteverdi specifically, it was pretty obvious to everyone whom he was complaining about.

Monteverdi didn't seem to mind; he went on composing just the same. A few years later, Artusi published another attack, this time naming names.

Monteverdi wasn't about to give in. Quite the contrary. He went so far as to develop a whole new style of music, which marked the beginning of opera. His music drama *Orfeo*, of 1607, could be considered the first true opera, although the idea had come from the earlier writings of Vincenzo Galilei (father of the astronomer Galileo), who was the champion of what he called the "representative style."

Galilei thought that this style of composition was a return to the ancient Greek ideals of music. He had no proof for this the-

[4] Does this sound familiar?

ory, since he had no real indication of what Greek music sounded like. But the idea sounded impressive.

The year 1607 was a good one in other respects: the Italians were just beginning to understand the proper use of forks at the dinner table. Things were looking up.

A big break for Monteverdi came in 1610, when he got the plum job of *maestro di cappella* at St. Mark's, the biggest and richest church in Venice. He was paid 300 ducats a year, which was more money than he'd ever seen in his life, and 100 ducats more than the previous *maestro* had got.

The job kept him busy. He supervised a choir of about 50 singers and instrumentalists and had to prepare and compose music for some 40 major church festivals each year.[5] Venetians knew how to party, and everyone went there for a good time. Sort of like Las Vegas.

Monteverdi loved his new job, which offered him creative status and a steady income. When the Mantuan duke tried to offer him his old job back, Monteverdi was quick to refuse.[6]

It's just as well he didn't return to Mantua. Not long afterwards, members of the Gonzaga family and the imperial army got into an argument over who should have control of the dukedom. The whole city was sacked and the soldiers infected everybody with plague. It was no longer a fun place to be.

Monteverdi escaped the plague, but old age finally got him when he was 75. The city clerk got his age wrong on the death certificate, but it was too late to make any difference.

[5] On Ascension Day, a party of officials went out to sea in the doge's *bucintoro*, or barge, and threw a big wedding ring into the water, symbolizing Venice's "marriage" to the sea.
[6] Roughly translated from the Italian, Monteverdi's reply was, "You've got to be kidding!"

VIVALDI

ANTONIO VIVALDI (1678-1741) IS CONSIDERED one of the foremost Italian composers of the Baroque era. He was famous, well respected and made a comfortable living most of his life, but he died a pauper. That's the way it goes.

Vivaldi might take some offence at being called an Italian, since he was actually born and lived in Venice. At that time Venice was a separate city-state, so Vivaldi was technically a Venetian, not an Italian. Maintaining the distinction between Venetians and Italians is something that you had to be a Venetian to be really good at. Nowadays, it's virtually a lost art.

When little Antonio was born, the midwife who delivered him baptized him right way. She wasn't at all sure he'd make it and wanted to give him a fighting chance at the Pearly Gates. He did survive, although he remained sickly all of his life.

Vivaldi's mother, Camilla, was a simple tailor's daughter and his father, Gianbattista, was a barber and also a talented violinist. He had three sisters, and two brothers who were always getting into trouble.[1]

Vivaldi studied for the priesthood and finally made it, although it took him nearly ten years to get around to all the various stages of the holy orders. Even after he became a full-fledged priest he hardly ever said mass. He claimed that his weak health — an asthmatic condition — made it too difficult for him. Some biographers prefer to believe that he could never get through a whole mass in one sitting because he was always dashing off to the sacristy to jot down a musical theme that had just popped into his head. Some biographers also have a theory that he was high up in the Venetian criminal

---

[1] His brother Francesco was banished for making faces at a bigshot.

underworld. There's no need to take this theory seriously.[2]

Because of the color of his hair, Vivaldi was nicknamed *Il prete rossa*, or "the red priest." Today he might be called "carrot-head."

Vivaldi spent most of his life as a teacher of violin at the *Ospedale della Pieta*, which was a school for orphaned girls. The Pieta was built in 1348, one of four institutions in the city built to house foundlings, orphans and other destitute children. There must have been a lot of these, since the original building was expanded several times over the centuries before Vivaldi came to teach there.

Today he might be called "carrot-head."

The Pieta was intended exclusively for girls and young women, many of whom were the illegitimate offspring of concubines and mistresses of the wealthy and powerful. The orphanage was surrounded by a big stone wall with an iron gate. Beside the gate was a little nook in the wall, just big enough to hold a baby. The porter went out every morning to check for new arrivals. The gate also had a large, stern sign warning everyone that the babies they left in the nook had better be ones that they couldn't care for by themselves.

The vast majority of his music Vivaldi composed for his pupils at the orphanage, which had developed an orchestra that was renowned all over Europe. Every Sunday, the Pieta orchestra gave a recital, for which the chapel was usually packed. Since it was in a church, applause was not permitted. Instead, the audience members would show their appreciation by coughing or blowing their noses loudly.[3] Some of the orphanage girls came to be quite celebrated for their musical ability.

Vivaldi himself was gaining quite a reputation, both as a violinist and as a composer. As well as teaching at the Pieta he played fiddle in the opera-house orchestra and sometimes filled in as music director at the orphanage for Francesco

---

[2] Nor the theory that he was a eunuch. The argument doesn't stand up.
[3] It's the same today.

Gasparini, who had a habit of disappearing on occasion.[4]

Venice in Vivaldi's time was an exciting place to be. There was music everywhere: even the lowliest cobblers and fruit vendors would whistle tunes in the marketplace. Gondoliers would burst into song at the least provocation.[5]

But the Venetians were an odd lot: there was nothing they liked more that spending vast amounts of money on expensive and elaborate clothing. They passed strict laws limiting the number of days when you were allowed to dress up. In 1732 the state passed a law prohibiting fans that were too luxurious. In 1750 it passed a law that ladies visiting each other could serve refreshments worth no more than a ducat.

The porter went out every morning to check for new arrivals

Nevertheless, visitors flocked to the city each year to take part in the famous Carnival festivities. Kings and queens, dukes, duchesses and other members of European nobility came for visits and went to parties, concerts and opera performances. When Frederick IV of Denmark and Norway visited Venice for the Carnival of 1708. He introduced himself to everybody as the Count of Olenburg, just so he could avoid all that bowing and scraping that kings usually have to put up with. He was so taken with the beauty of Venetian women that he had 12 miniature portraits painted of his favorites to carry around with him.

The Crown Prince and Princess of Russia caused quite a

---

[4] One day in 1713 he took a leave of absence and never came back.
[5] Vivaldi might have found this distracting. He didn't go out much.

commotion during their visit when they refused to pay half their hotel bill.[6]

In 1713, Vivaldi turned his hand to composing operas, 49 of which survive today. His first opera was *Ottone in villa*, with a libretto by Domenico Lalli. (Lalli's real name was Sebastino Biancardi, but he changed it after leaving Naples accused of embezzlement.) These operas were written between 1713 and 1739, for an average of nearly two each year.[7] His record time was the opera *Tito Manilo*, composed in only five days. He says so himself on the frontispiece. Vivaldi once boasted that he composed faster than a copyist could write down the music. He saved time by using shortcuts. In the manuscript of one of his violin concertos he gave up writing out the figured bass part and marked a section he'd already done with the comment, "for the dimwits."

Going to an 18th-century Venetian opera was definitely more fun if you were rich. Rich people sat in private boxes, where they could gamble and have food brought in. They had great fun dropping orange peels and spitting on the people below them, often aiming to put out their candles.

Opera singers posed their own particular problems for the composer. The famous castrato Luigi Marchesi, for instance, insisted that no matter what character he was playing in whatever opera, his first entrance had to be from the top of a hill. It didn't matter to him if the opera had no need for a hill in its plot. Either he got a hill or he didn't sing. Wearing a plumed helmet and carrying a sword, shield and lance, Marchesi would enter, singing the aria *Mia speranza io pur vorrei*, which the composer Giuseppe Sarti had written especially for him.

Although Vivaldi's operas were very popular in his day and he also composed quite a lot of music for church use, he is best remembered now for his many concertos, most of them for violin and orchestra. Among the best-known of his orchestral concertos are those known as the *Four Seasons*. Even people who don't like "classical" music like Vivaldi's *Four Seasons*, so he must be doing something right.

All in all, Vivaldi composed about 450 concertos of one sort or another. People who find his music too repetitious are inclined to say that he wrote the same concerto 450 times. This is hardly fair: he wrote two concertos, 225 times each.

[6] They also didn't leave a tip.

[7] Vivaldi himself says he wrote 94 operas, so that figure may need revision.

BACH

J UST ABOUT EVERYBODY in the Bach family was a good musician, but nobody was better at it than Johann Sebastian. If you wanted to, you could trace the Bach family back through five generations.[1] But you still wouldn't find anybody to beat J.S. Various members of the Bach clan were organists, town pipers and instrumentalists in Thuringia, a small state in the eastern part of what is now Germany.[2] As far as being musicians, the Bachs had Thuringia pretty much sewn up.

The Bach family.

Johann Sebastian's great-great-grandfather, old Veit Bach, was a miller. He liked to play his lute while the millstones ground flour in the background. J.S. later said it probably

[1] And a lot of people do. It's probably good for a PhD.
[2] German political geography is confusing even now. Back then it was nearly impossible.

helped him to keep time.[3] Johann Sebastian's father, Johann Ambrosius, married Elizabeth Lämmerhirt, whose family were prosperous furriers and part-time mystics.[4]

Johann Ambrosius had a twin brother named Johann Christoph. They looked so much alike that not even their wives could tell them apart. Johann Ambrosius (or someone who looked just like him) and Elizabeth had three sons: Johann Christoph, Johann Jakob, and Johann Sebastian.[5]

Johann Sebastian was born on March 21, 1685 and baptized two days later at the little church of St. George in Eisenach. At last report, the church still stands, and the present pastor still refers to that historic event whenever he baptizes a new little baby in the same font. Maybe he figures it will give them something to work towards.

At age eight, little Sebastian was sent off to school, where he did considerably better than his brother Johann Jakob. He was a good singer and was one of those pupils who always knows the answers to everything.[6] Probably no one else liked him very much.

His mother died when he was nine and his father a year later, so Sebastian was shipped off to the little town of Ohrdruf to live with his brother Johann Christoph, who was an organist and a pupil of Johann Pachelbel — the one who wrote the famous Canon.[7] Since money was scarce it was soon decided to send little Sebastian to the choir school of St Michael in Lüneberg. The rules stated that the singers had to be the "offspring of poor people, with nothing to live on, but possessing good voices." He seemed to qualify on all counts, so off he went.

The school paid for his tuition, room and board, and gave him candles and firewood. When his voice broke, we are told, Sebastian sang and spoke in octaves for a week. It must have been an interesting effect, but it didn't last. Anyway, Sebastian was kept busy after that playing violin, viola, and organ.

One of the ways Bach learned about music was to copy the compositions of his predecessors. He did a lot of this while at school. Nowadays we would call this plagiarism, but back then

[3] Veit had escaped to Thuringia from Hungary, where they frown on that sort of thing.
[4] Don't forget them. They'll turn up later.
[5] In the Bach family, you weren't anybody unless your name was Johann.
[6] You know the type.
[7] That's it. That's the only mention it's getting.

it must have been OK. Since photocopiers had not been invented yet, he had to do this by hand. Historian Cecil Gray says:
"He absorbed all styles, instead of being absorbed by them."
Karl Geiringer says something similar: "Young Sebastian
absorbed all instruction as readily as a sponge does water."[8]

For a while, Bach studied organ in Lüneberg with Georg
Böhm, who had been a pupil of a man named J.A. Reinken. Bach
walked 30 miles to Hamburg to hear Reinken play.[9] After arriv-
ing in Hamburg, Bach was hungry and tired from his long walk,
but had no money for a meal. As he tells the story, he was just
sitting outside an inn minding his own business, thinking about
food and rubbing his tired feet, when out from an open window
were tossed two herring heads. And as if that weren't enough,
each fish head contained a Danish ducat. Now *you* tell one.

*The coins-in-the-fish
trick.*

Having studied hard and soaked up
everything, it was time for Bach to get a
real job. His first position was as organist
and choirmaster of the little church of St.
Bonifacius in Arnstadt. The choir members, all boys, weren't very good singers
and were very rowdy. The young Bach
had trouble keeping them in line. His
bullish temper didn't help matters. He
once got into a street brawl with one of
his choristers, a boy named Geyersbach,
who called Bach a "dirty dog."[10]

A little later, Bach asked permission
from his employers to travel to Lübeck to hear the great Danish
organist Dietrich Buxtehude. They weren't terribly keen on the
idea, but they gave him four weeks off anyway. Bach set out,
again on foot.[11] It was more than 200 miles, but he made it
somehow.[12]

Bach had a wonderful time in Lübeck and was thrilled to
bits by Buxtehude's playing. Since Buxtehude was thinking of

---

[8] I'm sure these people mean well, but I don't think it's very polite to call
someone a sponge.
[9] As you'll soon find out, he was just warming up for the big Lübeck event.
[10] Bach had it coming to him. He had earlier called Geyersbach a
Zippelfagottist, or "nanny-goat bassoonist."
[11] Maybe he was hoping for a repeat of the coins-in-the-fish trick.
[12] Playing organ pedals must be good for the leg muscles.

retiring, he offered his job to Bach, who was 20. The only catch was that Bach had to marry Buxtehude's daughter Anna Margreta, who was nearly 30.[13] This seemed perfectly reasonable to Buxtehude, since he had done exactly the same thing to get the job from his predecessor, Franz Tunder.[14] Bach, however, was not so thrilled by the offer. He said thanks but no thanks. Two other great musicians of the time — Johann Matheson and George Frideric Handel — also turned down the offer of the job complete with wife. It wasn't the sort of fringe benefit they had in mind.[15]

What with one thing and another, Bach spent four months in Lübeck. When he got back to Arnstadt the church authorities were a bit angry, to put it mildly. Furthermore, Bach had come back with all sorts of fancy ideas about playing hymn tunes with lots of extra notes and ornamentation. This annoyed the congregation, since they had trouble finding the melody.[16] They told him to cut it out and keep things simple. So he did. *Too* simple.[17]

Bach wasn't keen on Buxtehude's daughter because he'd had his eye on someone closer to home. Very close to home, in fact. Her name was Maria Barbara Bach and she was his second cousin on his father's side. She was an orphan, living with her aunt and uncle in a little house called "The Golden Crown." Bach lived there for a while too, and that's how they met. It was convenient, anyway. She was cute as a button and had a lovely soprano voice. Pretty soon the church authorities noticed that the two of them were spending a lot of time alone together up in the organ loft. They were only practising their music, but that sort of thing makes church people nervous.[18]

So all things considered, Bach decided it might be a good idea to move somewhere else. He and Maria Barbara got married and moved to Mühlhausen and a new church job. Bach's salary in Mühlhausen was 85 *gulden* a year and "3 measures of

---

[13] It was a package deal.

[14] There's one born every minute.

[15] I know you're dying to know: the job (and the daughter) eventually went to a man named Johann Christian Schieferdecker. He didn't amount to much.

[16] Nobody likes a showoff.

[17] That will teach them to meddle with genius.

[18] At least that's what they *said* they were doing.

corn, 2 trusses of wood, one of beech, one of oak or aspen, and 6 trusses of faggots, delivered at his door, in lieu of arable."[19]

When the young couple were married, they were helped along financially by an inheritance from Tobias Lämmerhirt, Bach's uncle on his mother's side. Fourteen years later, in 1721, when Maria Barbara had died and Bach was about to be married again, he got an inheritance for the widow of Tobias Lämmerhirt.[20]

Things didn't work out very well in Mühlhausen. The church authorities were a sour-faced old bunch who didn't believe in having any fun. Within a year, Bach had accepted a job as court organist to Wilhelm Ernst, "His Ducal and Serene Highness of Saxe-Weimar." The duke offered Bach double his previous salary and Bach said "When do I begin?"[21] Bach's letter of resignation to the authorities at Mühlhausen starts like this: "Your Magnificence, Honored and Noble Sirs, Honored and Learned Sirs, Honored and Wise Sirs, Most Gracious Patrons and Gentlemen."[22] It gets worse.

The duke was a kind man, if somewhat stern. Everybody had to turn out all the lights by 8 p.m. (9 p.m. in the summer), and the duke had a habit of asking the servants at random about the subject of the chaplain's sermons. He wanted to make sure they'd been awake. The duke liked music and the organ at Weimer was a good one, but the first thing Bach did was to install a set of chimes. Then it was even better.[23]

All the years of practice, not to mention the walking tours, had made Bach into a terrific organist. Once when playing a concert at the royal court of Cassel, he played an elaborate pedal solo so well that the crown prince took a ring off his finger and presented it to Bach. As one observer put it: "If the skill of his feet alone earned him such a gift, what might the Prince have given him had he used his hands as well?"[24]

---

[19] I don't know whether he was paid in corn and firewood all at once, or little bits every two weeks, or what. Someone should look into it.

[20] It was a good thing he didn't marry a third time. He was running out of Lämmerhirts.

[21] The salary was double the money. I'm not sure about the firewood.

[22] He didn't want to leave anyone out.

[23] Bach thought there was nothing like a good set of chimes.

[24] Maybe the prince was just as easy to impress. He probably gave a ring to every Tom, Dick and Johann who passed by.

But through it all Bach remained the same humble man he'd always been. When someone complimented him on his playing. he once said: "There's nothing to it. You have only to hit the right notes at the right time and the instrument plays itself." That's easy for *him* to say.[25]

Along about this time, Bach became friends with Johann Gottfried Walther, an organist and lexicographer.[26] He also won a public clavier-playing contest against the great French keyboard player Louis Marchand, who failed to show up. On the day of the contest, Marchand suddenly remembered he had important business out of town. You know how it is.

Bach spent nearly 10 years at Weimar, but then found it was time to move on. The old duke was having a family quarrel with his nephew and Bach was sort of caught in the middle. So he accepted a job at the court of Prince Leopold of Anhalt-Cöthen. Bach didn't leave on the best of terms. He spent nearly a month in jail "for too obstinately requesting his dismissal." While he was under arrest he composed 46 chorale preludes, so the time wasn't completely wasted.[27]

At Cöthen, Bach had a 17-piece orchestra, which kept him busily composing. The court bookbinders finally had to ask him to slow down so they could catch up. He composed little instruction books for his son Wilhelm Friedemann. (The boy, we are told, was very bright, just like his dad. Historians know this because he used to doodle a lot on his school books. Maybe he was just bored.) If you wanted to, you could think of Bach's children by Maria Barbara as his second cousins once removed. But that's probably not a good idea.

Bach tried out for an organist job at the Jacobkirche in Hamburg and although he dazzled the judges with his playing, they wouldn't give him the job unless he made a hefty "donation" to the church. Bach refused and the job went to a second-rate organist named Johann Joachim Heitmann, who just happened to have a spare 4,000 marks in his pockets.[28]

---

[25] Historian Dr. Charles Burney tells us that Bach sometimes used a stick in his mouth to hit a key he couldn't reach with either hand.

[26] They were cousins. Walther was a Lämmerhirt on his mother's side.

[27] The Weimar Council snubbed him later, too. When they came to publish a list of court organists over the years, they left Bach out completely.

[28] The same sort of thing was expected if you applied for the job of Council Cake Baker.

Later, Bach composed a set of six concertos that he sent as a gift to Christian Ludwig, The Margrave of Brandenburg.[29] Bach copied out the score very neatly, tied it up with a nice ribbon and sent it off to him. The margrave thanked him very much but probably never opened the package. He didn't have an orchestra, so it didn't do him much good to have the music. Well, it's the thought that counts.

After Maria Barbara died, Bach married again, this time to Anna Magdalena Wülcken, who at 20 was 16 years younger than he was. She was a very good singer and a good copyist besides. After a while of copying Bach's manuscripts, her handwriting began to look like his. Maybe she wrote some of the music: who knows?

Bach's patron, Prince Leopold, got married at about this time, too, but he didn't do as well. His new wife was his cousin the Princess of Anhalt-Bernberg and she thought music was a waste of time. She liked to do needlework, but it's not the same somehow.

So in 1723, Bach and his new wife packed up all their possessions and the kiddies (there were seven by this time, four boys and three girls) and moved to Leipzig, where Bach was appointed cantor and music director of the *Thomasschule*.

Bach's possessions included six claviers, a lute and several other instruments; a variety of candlesticks; two silver coffeepots, one large, one small; a silver teapot; and assorted pieces of furniture. He also had three different coats (the silk one was somewhat worn, he says) and 11 linen shirts "at the wash." He probably picked them up before he left town.

11 linen shirts "at the wash"

At the St. Thomas School, Bach was expected to teach the boys music, Latin, and grammar, while leading "a sober and secluded life." He hired a man named Petzoldt to teach his Latin classes for him.[30]

Bach was busy at Leipzig. When not disciplining small boys he found the time to compose nearly 300 cantatas, the *B-minor Mass*, and his mighty *St. Matthew Passion* (we

[29] You don't hear of many margraves anymore. I wonder why?
[30] Can't say I blame him.

can argue about the *St. John Passion*, too, if you'd like). In his spare moments he composed other things. His old temper hadn't left him: when the university officials turned down Bach's application to compose a special piece of music and gave the job instead to a man named Görner, Bach tossed his wig at him and said he would have made a better cobbler. Bach's salary at the school was 700 *thaler* a year, with extra money to lead the choir for funerals.[31]

The school's old rector died, and was replaced by Johann August Ernesti. He was one of those progressive types who didn't care for music much. He used to call the boys in the school orchestra "pot-house fiddlers," which was bad for morale. Bach spent more and more time travelling around the country-side trying out new organs, as an excuse to get away.

In his last years, Bach was nearly blind and his health was declining. It was all he could do to jot down the first 239 bars of the last fugue of *The Art of Fugue*, the most amazingly com-plicated fugal composition ever written. An English oculist, John Taylor, attempted surgery on Bach's eyes but it did no good: the operation left him completely blind. Suddenly, on July 18, 1750, Bach's eyesight was miraculously restored, but he suffered a stroke and died 10 days later.[32]

Anna Magdalena never remarried and tried to struggle along on a measly pension. She died a bag lady in the streets of Leipzig. Wilhelm Friedemann did pretty well as a composer and recitalist. One source tells us that "he had a beautifully shaped long-fingered hand."[33] Carl Philipp Emanuel worked for Frederick the Great, King of Prussia. Frederick liked to play flute, but took liberties with the tempo. C.P.E. just played along and said nothing. After all, Frederick was the king. Johann Christian moved to London and wrote operas.

There were other Bachs but none of them amounted to much. Bach's grandson, Johann Sebastian II, was a painter, but you can't get ahead that way. By May of 1871, historian Sanford Terry says, "Bach's blood had ceased to flow in mortal veins."[34]

---

[31] Bach complained in a letter to his friend Erdmann that people in Leipzig just weren't dying fast enough for him to make a decent living.

[32] He probably took a look at his doctor's bills.

[33] But it doesn't say which hand, left or right.

[34] And once the blood stops, you've had it.

HANDEL

IF ANYONE HAD KNOWN THAT Handel was going to grow up to become such a great composer, maybe we would know more about his early life. But nobody was paying much attention at the time.[1]

George Frideric Handel was born in 1685 in the little town of Halle, in Saxon Germany. If you go to Halle today, you'll see a house with a sign that says "Handel's birthplace." He was born in the house next door.

Handel's grandfather, Valentin Händel, had moved to Halle about 1600 and became the town's official bread weigher. His father, Georg, who was 62 when the boy was born, was a prominent barber and surgeon. That's a useful combination of trades, although customers had to be careful when they asked Georg to take a little off the top and sides. But at least if he cut you shaving he knew how to stitch you back up again. He once removed part of a knife blade from a boy who had swallowed it a year and a half earlier. Georg just looped a string around it and pulled. The boy came to be known as Rudolff the Sword Swallower.

Handel's father had no interest in music, so he thought his son shouldn't either.[2] He wanted his son to become a lawyer and make something of himself.[3] Handel's mother Dorothea, was more tolerant and the story goes that she smuggled a small, quiet keyboard instrument called a clavichord into the house so the boy could practise late at night in the attic while his father was asleep. The story sounds too good to be true, if

---

[1] Next time we'll know better.
[2] People are funny that way.
[3] Music is full of people who might have become lawyers. It never seems to happen the other way around.

you ask me, Handel probably made it up.[4]

One day when he was about nine, Handel went with his father to the palace of the duke, who wanted more curls and a little trim at the back. While Handel's father was busy snipping, the boy wandered into a chapel where there was an organ. Forgetting his manners, he started to play some of the music he'd been practising in the attic. Fortunately, the duke wasn't angry, and made Handel's father promise to give the boy music lessons. So he studied organ with a man named Zachau.

Handel practised late at night.

Handel enrolled at the University of Halle at 17 to study law. His father had died earlier that year, but he went ahead with law anyway, even though his heart wasn't in it. He preferred concertos to codicils any old day.[5] Still, it was a thoughtful gesture for the old man. Pretty soon, however, Handel jumped at a chance to become an organist at the Halle cathedral and left school. He had already filled in many times before for the regular organist, who often arrived too drunk to play.

By 1703 Handel had left Halle for the big city of Hamburg, where he supported himself teaching private students and play-

[4]In some versions it is his aunt Anna who gave him the instrument. But why complicate matters?
[5]But you should see his will. It has more codicils than you can shake a stick at.

ing second violin in the opera-house orchestra.[6] He became friends with Johann Matheson and the two travelled to Lübeck to meet the great Danish organist Dietrich Buxtehude. He offered them each his job in return for marrying his daughter. They said they'd think about it and then left town in a hurry.[7]

Handel and Matheson also got into a big quarrel once, which they settled by having a rapier duel. It might have been serious when Handel was stabbed, but Matheson's sword was stopped by a button on Handel's coat. After that, they made up and were friends again, although Handel took to wearing coats with extra-large buttons all over.

Handel's first two operas were produced in Hamburg: they were a moderate success. But Handel knew that if he wanted to make it in big-time opera, Italy was where it's at. He went there in 1706, although it's not at all clear where he got the money to afford it.[8]

Handel spent most of 1707 in Rome, even though there wasn't any opera going on. The Pope had banned opera as being offensive and sacrilegious.[9] Even though there was no opera, Handel had a good time anyway, with lots of parties and musical events. He met many important Italian composers of the day, such as Archangelo Corelli and the Scarlattis — Alessandro and his son Domenico.

Handel and the younger Scarlatti had a little contest to see who was the better player. Scarlatti beat him at the harpsichord but Handel cleaned up on the organ, so it worked out to a tie.

Handel played tourist for a while and went off to Venice. In 1709 his opera *Agrippina* was performed there. The audience loved it so much that they began shouting "*Viva il caro Sassone*," which means "Long live the beloved Saxon." Handel was in and he knew it.[10] All told, Handel spent about three years in Italy. In addition to the operas, he wrote about 100 cantatas and some church music. And had a good time.

In 1710, Handel accepted a job as *Kapellmeister* to the

[6] Handel didn't enjoy playing second fiddle to anyone. But it was a living.
[7] The same thing happened to Bach, remember?
[8] Maybe it's better not to ask.
[9] He'd get into a snit like that every so often and the only thing to do was to humor him.
[10] He was a little worried at first. He thought they were calling him a sissy.

Elector of Hanover. He got the job because he knew someone who knew someone.[11] He had only been there a few months when he asked for some time off to go to London. On his way he passed through Halle and said "Hi" to his mom, who told him to pack clean socks and write home when he got the chance.

Handel was an even bigger hit in England than he'd been in Italy. Londoners accepted him with great enthusiasm. They hadn't had any composer to get really excited about since the death of Purcell back in 1695, so Handel came along at just the right time.

He composed the opera *Rinaldo* for his first London visit and the crowds loved it. Whole chunks of *Rinaldo* are made up of music Handel took from his earlier opera *Agrippina* and some other oratorios, but the audiences didn't know that. And Handel wasn't about to tell them.[12] One of the highlights of *Rinaldo* is his use of recorders to represent singing birds. And in case that didn't get the point across, at every performance there were a few live sparrows released on stage. This sort of thing is all right as long as it doesn't get out of hand.[13]

Eventually, Handel realized that he had better keep his promise to return to his job in Hanover, although he didn't want to. Compared to London, life at the court of Hanover was dull. Within a year, he had convinced the elector to let him visit London again, promising to return in a "reasonable" time. His first London visit had lasted seven months. This next one lasted nearly 50 years.[14]

Handel composed a couple of operas for the 1712 season and also a birthday ode for Queen Anne, his first setting of English words. He hadn't quite got the hang of the language, but was keen to work at it.

In 1713, Owen MacSwiney, manager of the Haymarket Theatre, skipped town with all the money from Handel's opera *Teseo*. It put a strain on their relationship.

In 1714, Queen Anne died and Handel's boss the Elector of

---

[11] It's the same today.

[12] Handel often borrowed from his own music. Later he got a little carried away and started stealing from other composers, too.

[13] One of his later operas included live bears.

[14] You know how it is: you lose track of time.

Hanover (surprise, surprise!) became King George I of England. He couldn't speak a word of English, but that didn't seem to bother anybody, least of all George. He never knew what anyone was talking about, but that didn't seem to be a requirement of the job.

A lot of people seem to think that George was angry at Handel for having run off on him and the story goes that Handel composed the orchestral suite known as the *Water Music* to get back on George's good side. George wasn't angry at all. One of the first things he did when he arrived was to give Handel a raise. The king also went to a performance of Handel's opera *Rinaldo*. He was supposed to be in disguise, but he brought along his favorite mistress and they chattered in German through the whole performance, so everyone knew who it was.

The players got a little wet.

There's no doubt that George enjoyed the *Water Music*, which Handel composed for a special royal outing on the Thames. The king and his friends floated down the river eating and drinking, while Handel and 50 musicians floated beside them on another barge, playing dance music.[15] The king liked the music so much that he had it played three times. It was a huge success, although the players got a little wet.

Handel moved to Middlesex for a while as a house guest of James Brydges, the Duke of Chandos. Chandos had been pay-

---

[15] How Handel expected anyone to dance on a barge I don't know.

master to Queen Anne's army during the War of the Spanish Succession and somehow came out of it a whole lot richer than when he went in.[16] He spent a fortune building a big house called Cannons, which had plenty of guest rooms. Handel composed the 11 church anthems now known as the *Chandos Anthems* while he was there. One story tells us that during a thunderstorm Handel took refuge in a village blacksmith's shop and then composed a set of variations on a tune he heard the "Harmonious Blacksmith" whistling. You can believe it if you like.

In 1719, a group of noblemen set up the Royal Academy of Music and asked Handel to be music director. They wanted to produce great operas, so Handel went off to Europe to hire singers. Handel dropped in to Halle to see his mother. Hearing he was in town, Bach walked the 20 miles from Leipzig to meet him, but by the time Bach arrived Handel had just left.

Opera in the 18th century was quite different from nowadays. Back then, the audience didn't even *pretend* to be listening to the music. They went to socialize, play cards, eat and flirt with whomever caught their fancy. The singers didn't help matters. They would bring their favorite arias with them and insert them into the action, even if the aria was from a different opera.

The leading female role (called a *prima donna*) was usually a soprano. The leading male was usually a castrato from Italy, where they specialize in that sort of operation and have sharper knives. He was called a *primo uomo*.[17] Tenors were rarely used, and never for important parts.[18] The music consisted mostly of arias, about 30 of them, in the *da capo* form with a built-in repeat. It was like having a guaranteed encore.

The Royal Academy opened in 1720 and Handel set to work composing one opera after another. Audiences created a bit of rivalry between Handel and another composer, Bononcini. But it was nothing compared to the rivalry over the two main sopranos, Cuzzoni and Faustina.

Handel had brought Cuzzoni from Italy.[19] She was a bit

---

[16] Thrifty management, obviously.

[17] And something else behind his back.

[18] Those were the good old days.

[19] He sent Sandoni, one of the orchestra players, to escort her. By the time they arrived back in London they were married.

moody but had a lovely voice. Horace Walpole describes her as "short and squat." Once when she disagreed with the way Handel wanted her to sing an aria, he held her out of the window until she saw things his way.

Handel was always having trouble with singers. When a tenor named Gordon threatened to jump on Handel's harpsichord, the composer said: "Tell me when and I will advertise. More people will come to see you jump than to hear you sing." That shut him up.

In order to draw larger crowds, the academy imported another soprano, named Faustina. Her rivalry with Cuzzoni went to absurd lengths. For one opera, Handel had to compose two arias, one for each of them, with an equal number of notes so that neither singer would feel cheated.

The rivalry came to head in 1727, during the performance of Bononcini's opera *Astianatto*. Different factions of the audience hissed and cheered for their favorite of the two singers. The audience got so heated that a fight broke out, followed by one on stage, with the two sopranos going at each other tooth and nail. Some people take their entertainment very seriously.

That same year, George I died from eating too many melons and was succeeded by his son George II.[20] For his coronation, Handel composed the anthem *Zadok The Priest*, which has been sung at every coronation ever since. But George got it first.

In 1729, Handel made another trip to Italy to find good singers and came back with a soprano named Anna Maria Strada del Po. She remained loyal to him even when business was bad and all his other singers deserted him for a rival opera company, The Opera of the Nobility.

There has been some speculation that Handel and Strada might have been having an affair, but I find no evidence to support this theory.[21] In fact, not much is known about Handel's love life. He never married, although he did seem to have an eye for the ladies. (There was one he toured Europe with as a young man, but I forget her name.) Historian Stanley Sadie puts it this way: "A composer who could depict women in his music as vividly as Handel does is unlikely to have been entirely ignorant of them in real life." Well, that's tactful.

---

[20] George II did no better. When he died he was sitting on the toilet.
[21] Her nickname was "The Pig."

At some point in any discussion of Handel, his oratorio *Messiah* is bound to come up. Oratorio was a useful escape for Handel from the problems associated with opera. In many ways the music is the same, but without all the trouble of scenery and costumes and movement. On the whole, oratorio is a lot cheaper to produce than opera, which must have appealed to Handel's strong business sense.[22]

Handel composed *Messiah* in just under three weeks. That's fast but nowhere close to the record, even for him.[23] The libretto was compiled by Charles Jennens, who was a good librettist but an extravagant fop. He had one servant whose job it was to pick up the oyster shells that Jennens discarded after him everywhere he went.

On his way to the Dublin premiere of *Messiah*, Handel stopped off in Chester and assembled a bunch of singers to run through some of the new choruses. One of the basses, a printer named Janson, made so many mistakes that Handel raged at him: "I thought you told me you could read music at sight!"

"Yes sir, and so I can," Janson replied. "But not at *first* sight."

Messiah was first performed in 1742, with 700 people packed into a theatre designed to hold 600. In the advertisements, ladies were asked to wear skirts without hoops and gentlemen were asked to leave their swords at home to make more room. It was a huge success and later caught on in London, where Handel used it to close the season with a bang each year.

Handel, of course, was something of an expert on big, showy music. He once told the composer Gluck: "What the English like is something they can beat time to, something that hits them straight in the eardrum."[24]

As anyone will tell you, the king was so moved by the first London performance of the *Hallelujah* chorus that he stood up, thereby establishing a silly tradition that continues to this day. Personally, I think his foot had gone to sleep. You might call it the musical version of the seventh-inning stretch.

---

[22] He was also discouraged at having to set such awful librettos to music. The high point of *Serse*, for instance, is the hero's love song to a tree.

[23] He composed his opera *Faramondo* in nine days. But it shows.

[24] We must remember, however, that Handel once said of Gluck that he "knows no more of counterpoint than my cook."

Speaking of big bangs, that was the theory behind Handel's *Royal Fireworks Music*. The king had arranged for a big party with fireworks and music to celebrate with. But the special platform holding the fireworks caught fire and everything went off too early. Then it rained. After the smoke had cleared, two people were dead and hundreds injured. But the music was nice.

By this time, Handel was old and extremely fat and losing his eyesight. His sight only got worse after surgery by John Taylor, who deserves a place in history for having ruined the eyes of the two greatest composers of the period, Bach and Handel, and also of historian Edward Gibbon.[25]

Handel died on Good Friday in 1759 and was buried in Westminster Abbey among all the poets. You'd think that with all the music he composed someone would have had the sense to have some of it performed at his funeral. But the funeral music was composed by William Croft. Handel got his revenge later. No one listens to Croft nowadays.

[25] It shows what you can do if you apply yourself.

SOME CLASSIC EXAMPLES

HAYDN

HAYDN HAD NEITHER THE flashy individuality of Mozart nor the brooding, romantic passion of Beethoven. He was more of a middle-management type.

Haydn did spend a few years struggling to make ends meet as a young man in Vienna.[1] But he spent most of his life — nearly 50 years — at the same job, which offered him creative scope and financial security. He was 24 years older than Mozart yet outlived him by 18 years. And until his very last years he enjoyed, unlike Beethoven, good health.

More of a middle-management type

He spent his final years in well-deserved, peaceful retirement, in comfortable surroundings and with a private stock of his favorite wine, a tokay. Haydn died in 1809 at 77 years of age,

[1]He lived in a garret and everything.

with money in the bank and a wardrobe full of nice clothes. If his love life had gone better, he would have been even happier.[2]

Haydn was born into a simple peasant family in the little Austrian village of Rohrau, near the border with Hungary, in 1732. His father was a second-generation wheelwright and his mother was a cook. they christened their son Franz Joseph, but around the house they called him "Sepperl."

As a boy he was well-mannered and tidy. He liked to pretend he was playing the fiddle on two sticks of firewood. Well, it's a start.

When he was six, he went to live with a schoolmaster cousin in the nearby town of Hainburg. This man, Franck, was a stern teacher who thought that his pupils could learn anything if only he beat them often enough.[3] Haydn did learn from him, at least enough to be accepted as a choirboy at St. Stephen's cathedral in Vienna. He was auditioned by the choirmaster, George Reutter, who bribed him with cherries and taught him how to sing a trill. Haydn said much later in life that he could never hear a trill without thinking of the taste of cherries.[4]

Little Haydn was a good singer but a bit of a prankster. One prank finally lost him his place: he snipped the pigtail off the boy in front of him and Reutter kicked him out of the choir. It was just as well: his voice was beginning to break and there was talk of castrating him. So there he was, 17 years old with just three worn shirts, a ragged jacket and no money to his name.

For the next few years, Haydn lived a gypsy life as one of the many street musicians, or buskers, in the city of Vienna. He made a little extra money giving music lessons, just enough to pay the rent at his tiny garret on the *Michaelerplaz*. Late at night he studied the keyboard works of C.P.E. Bach and composed his own music.

His first big break came when he and some fellow buskers serenaded the house of Johann Joseph Kurz, a comedian and pantomime performer popularly known as Kurz-Bernardon, after his most famous role. Bernardon is a stock comic character, a simpleton also known as Hanswurst.[5] Kurz commissioned

---

[2] There's always a catch, isn't there?
[3] He also gambled with loaded dice.
[4] Pavlov would be proud of him.
[5] Not to be confused with *bratwurst*, or *liverwurst*, or any other type of *wurst*.

Haydn to compose the music for a comic opera, *Der krumme Teufel* (The Crooked Devil). Haydn got paid 25 ducats, which made him feel very rich.[6]

After that, things started looking up for Haydn. The court poet Metastasio lived in a nicer apartment in the same building and through him Haydn met Niccolo Porpora, a famous singing teacher and composer. Haydn became his accompanist and valet. From Porpora he learned not only fundamentals of composition but also how to polish boots and keep the lint off a velvet jacket.

It was about this time that Haydn fell madly in love with one of his pupils, a lovely young woman named Therese Keller, a wigmaker's daughter. Haydn wanted to marry her, but she decided she wanted to become a nun instead. When she entered the convent in 1756 Haydn composed a little organ concerto for the ceremony, just to show that there were no hard feelings.

As a sort of consolation prize, Therese's father suggested that Haydn could marry her older sister, Anna Maria. She was 31, he was 28. Too upset to think straight, he said yes. He lived to regret it: Anna Maria was ugly, ill-tempered, and a bad housekeeper. Shortly into their marriage, she became a born-again Christian and spent all hours entertaining clergymen in their home. Worst of all, she had no appreciation of Haydn's life as a musician. She didn't care whether he was a cobbler or a composer. She would use his

Mrs. Haydn curling her hair.

manuscripts to line cake tins, or cut the paper into strips to curl her hair with.[7]

Haydn had a simple antidote to this suffering: he fooled around. He later said he felt little guilt about this, since his wife was unable to bear children.[8]

First he fell in love with a singer named Luiga Polzelli. They

---

[6]I'd hum you a few bars of the music, but it's been lost.
[7]As a final irony, Therese soon left the nunnery. But by then it was too late.
[8]I'm not sure I follow his logic, but I can't say that I blame him.

kept hoping her husband and his wife would die. Her husband did die, but Haydn's wife stuck around until 1800, when he was 68. Polzelli, meanwhile, had married someone else. Haydn's second love he met while visiting London, another singer, named Rebecca Schroeter. There were probably others.

Through his connection with Porpora, Haydn soon got a job as a composer to the court of Count Morzin, a Bohemian nobleman.[9] From there he was offered the job he stayed at for the rest of his life, as court composer and *Kapellmeister* to Prince Paul Anton Esterházy, a Hungarian nobleman.

Paul Anton didn't last long and was soon replaced by his brother, Nicolaus the Magnificent. Nicolaus was a kind man and a decent musician, even if he did have a penchant for flashy clothing.[10] Haydn's own uniform was blue with gold trim. Later it was red with gold trim.

Nicolaus liked to play an instrument called the baryton, which is a sort of cross between a cello and a guitar. Nobody makes them anymore. But if you wanted to learn it, Haydn wrote about 160 chamber pieces for the baryton, which ought to keep you busy for a while.[11]

Not content with the family palace at Eisenstadt, Nicolaus decided to build a splendid new summer castle, which he named Esterháza. He had it built in a swamp in the middle of nowhere because he was fond of duck hunting.[12]

Esterháza was a classy place, but Haydn and his musicians didn't like being stuck in the boondocks, so far away from Vienna, not to mention their wives and husbands. The quarters were mostly single rooms. Haydn had one of the few apartments with room for his wife, not that he spent any more time with her than he had to.

This situation led Haydn to compose one of his best-known symphonies, No. 45 in F-sharp minor, known as the *"Farewell" Symphony*. The joke comes at the end of the final movement,

---

[9]No, that's not a contradiction in terms: Bohemia was a country back then, not just an adjective.

[10]Goethe was particularly impressed by his diamond-studied hussar's uniform.

[11]Nicolaus was an easy man to please. When he got angry, a new baryton trio would cheer him up. If that didn't, two usually would.

[12]Haydn also liked fishing and hunting. He once felled three birds with one shot.

when as the instrumental parts drop away, each player was instructed to snuff out his candle and leave the stage. By the end there were only two violins playing, Haydn and Luigi Tomasini. Nicolaus got the message and everyone packed to leave the next day.

Haydn's compositions have more nicknames than those of any other composer in the history of music. When you consider that he wrote, for example, at least 22 symphonies in D major, the nicknames become useful. Altogether, he wrote about 107 symphonies,[13] a dozen masses, 52 piano sonatas and about 84 string quartets.[14] He had to have something to keep him out of the house at nights.

Even though his marriage was a disaster, Haydn had plenty else to be happy about. He was well respected by his contemporaries, including Mozart and Beethoven, who both studied with him.[15] The members of his orchestra all called him "Papa." He had stubby legs and a big nose and a mischievous sense of humor.[16]

When Haydn died in 1809, there was a simple funeral. since Austria was rather busy being invaded by Napoleon's troops. A couple of amateur medical students secretly stole Haydn's skull and put it in a little black box with a white silk cushion. They wanted to read the bumps on his head.

In 1829, Prince Nicolaus Esterházy II had the body exhumed. When he found that it had no head, boy was he mad! He finally tracked down the thieves and demanded it back. They had donated Hadyn's skull to a Viennese musical society and gave him some other skull instead. It wasn't until 1954 that Haydn's head was buried along with the rest of his body. Other than that, though, he was a pretty together guy.

[13]He stopped counting after that, and so have I.
[14]He didn't call them string quartets, but that's what they are.
[15]He charged Beethoven a nominal fee and let him pay for the coffee when they went out.
[16]He thought it was pretty funny when the Countess Morzin's blouse fell open as she turned the page during a lesson.

MOZART
....

MOZART IS JUST GOD'S WAY of making the rest of us feel insignificant. Whenever you have just composed a piece of music you think is particularly good, it is humbling to think that Mozart probably wrote a better one when he was nine years old.

January 27, 1756 was pretty much a day like any other, until about 8 p.m., when the greatest prodigy music has ever known was born to Leopold and Maria Anna Mozart, in a little third-floor apartment that they rented from a grocer.[1] The baby's name was Johannes Chrysostomus Wolfgangus Theophilus, but he preferred Wolfgang Amadeus.[2]

Little Wolfgang did not start out being particularly remarkable. In fact, for the first three years he was quite ordinary: he wet his pants, played with his food and slobbered on his shirt-front just the same as any other small child. Until he was nearly four he was a complete slacker — he didn't compose a note of music and hardly played the harpsichord at all. By age five he had rolled up his shirtsleeves and gotten down to some serious work. He became a whiz at the keyboard and began composing simple pieces. The sound of a solo trumpet would send him screaming from the room. He wasn't very fond of the flute, either.

At age nine he wrote his first choral piece, which is now in the British Museum. It is a setting of a verse from Psalm 46, "God is our refuge and strength."[3] He waited till he was 12 to

---

[1] The grocer's name was Johann Lorenz Hagenaur, but he doesn't matter at all in the rest of the story.

[2] Or probably "Wolfie" for short. He changed Theophilus to Amadeus, both of which mean "beloved of God." Who could argue?

[3] Mozart can be forgiven for calling this piece a "madrigal." He was still young and had a lot to learn.

compose his first opera, *La Finta Semplice*. From then on, there was no stopping him. In his short life of 36 years, Mozart composed half a dozen first-rate operas and several others, 21 piano concertos, 24 string quartets, 17 masses, assorted chamber music and other solo concertos, and 41 symphonies.[4]

Why was Mozart such an overachiever? Blame his father as much as anyone: Leopold was a nag, constantly berating his son to work hard, make money and above all not to hang around with other musicians.[5] But Mozart wasn't interested in hard work: he just wanted to have fun.

No doubt about it, Mozart was compulsive. Even as a small child this was true. When he was learning mathematics, he would fill the whole room — walls, floors, furniture — with numbers written with a piece of chalk.[6] His obsessive drive has its roots in the constant concert touring he gave as a small boy with his older sister, Anna Maria, known as "Nannerl." Leopold toured his children as performing prodigies to all the noble courts and big cities of Europe. On a visit to the French royal court, Mozart proposed marriage to Marie Antoinette. She turned him down.[7]

Marie Antoinette turned him down

On a visit to Rome when he was 14, Mozart wrote down the score of Allegri's *Miserere* after hearing the Sistine Chapel choir

[4]Give or take a few symphonies. I'm not going to quibble.
[5]Leo thought musicians had no class. Maybe he was right.
[6]His parents should be grateful that they lived before the invention of the felt-tip marker.
[7]They were both seven years old at the time.

perform it only once. The Pope had said that no one should write it down, but that didn't stop Mozart. Mendelssohn did the same thing about 70 years later, when he was 21.

In 1782, much against his father's wishes, Mozart married Constanze Weber, his landlady's daughter, whose older sister Aloysia had earlier jilted him. His father thought neither of the Weber daughters was good enough for him. Mozart, ever the soul of romance, wrote of Constanze in a letter to his father:

"She is not ugly but by no means a beauty. She is not witty but has enough sound common sense to enable her to fulfill her duties as a wife and mother."

Constanze was every bit as irresponsible as her childish husband, and their housekeeping was a constant mess. They moved 11 times in the nine years they lived in Vienna.[8] Much as they may have both flirted with others, they were in love and happy together. And that's all that counts.

Mozart never got the prestigious court appointment he knew he deserved. He worked for a while at the court of the Archbishop of Salzburg, until one day he got uppity with the archbishop's executive assistant, who kicked Mozart out — literally, right in the seat of the pants. His status in the archbishop's household was that of any other servant: composers were not considered any different from valets or serving girls. In a letter to his father, Mozart explains the etiquette of dining:

"By the way, the two valets sit at the top of the table, but at least I have the honor of being placed above the cooks."

Part of Mozart's problem was that he was abrasive and tactless in his opinions of fellow composers and others, both in his letters and in person. When the French philosopher Voltaire died, Mozart wrote: "That Godless arch-rascal Voltaire has pegged out like a dog, like a beast. That is his reward." People tend to resent that sort of comment.[9]

Making enough money was a constant struggle for Mozart, in part because for many of his commissions and concerts he was paid not in cash but with gifts. "No money but a fine gold watch," he writes in a letter. "What one needs on a journey is money; and let me tell you, I now have five gold watches." He

---

[8]When that wasn't enough, she would rearrange the furniture.
[9]He was rude, too. Reading his letters to his cousin Maria Anna Thekla would make you blush.

often borrowed money from his friend Michael Puchburg, who didn't seem to mind that he never paid it back.

Mozart's appointment to the court of the emperor Franz Joseph II paid him 800 *gulden* a year. This was more money than his father made but considerably less than the 2,000 *gulden* Gluck had been paid for the position. But Gluck did more work. Mozart's composing duties for the emperor were light. He regarded the salary as "too much for what I have done but too little for what I could do."

Mozart was placed above the cooks.

Many of his compositions were produced for particular occasions or as favors to his friends. Mozart wrote a serenade, for instance, for the wedding celebrations of the daughter of Sigmund Haffner, a wealthy Salzburg burgomaster.[10] Many of these pieces did not earn him much money, if any at all.

But really he had only himself to blame: he drank too much and gambled away most of his money on cards and billiards. And he was lousy at both.

[10]Haffner paid the archbishop a large annual sum to avoid scrutiny of his ledger books.

Everybody likes to think that Mozart died penniless and was buried in a pauper's grave. That's not exactly true. He did leave debts behind and his wife arranged for a simple funeral to save costs. After his death, she became very shrewd in business, keeping careful control of his manuscripts and arranging for their publication. She later married a diplomat and amateur musician, Georg Nikolaus Nissen, who wrote an early biography of the great composer.[11]

Constanze also did what she could to defend his reputation. Taking offence at some comments on Mozart by Schlichtegroll, she bought up an entire printing of the book and removed the offending passages.

There's also been a lot of loose talk that Mozart was poisoned by Salieri, a rival composer. You can believe it if you like. You're in good company with Pushkin and Rimsky-Korsakov, who made the whole story into an opera. I'd like to believe it too. Really I would. It makes a great story.

Mozart was a prodigy and a genius who set the standards for everyone else to follow. He started young, made a big splash, and died early, so that everyone could lament his unrealized potential. Any of you wishing to be considered prodigies or geniuses should live by his example.[12]

Mozart was short — about 5 foot, 4 inches — unattractive, abusive, temperamental and irresponsible. But he was a genius who wrote heart-cramping music that continues to be admired centuries after his death. It just goes to show that politeness isn't everything.

[11]Nissen's epitaph reads: "Here lies Mozart's widow's second husband." That's fame for you.
[12]The English composer William Crotch failed to learn the lesson of Mozart's life. Crotch, born in 1775, was a prodigy who gave concerts at age three and was a full professor of music at 22. He wrote his first oratorio at age 14. He died in 1847 at the ripe old age of 72, having grown consistently less remarkable as the years dragged on.

THOSE ROMANTIC
TYPES

BEETHOVEN

OF ALL THE GREAT COMPOSERS, Beethoven was probably the one most inclined to brood. He had plenty to brood about.[1] He was moody, bad-tempered, arrogant, and often insulting. But he could also be warm, affectionate and good-humored. You just had to catch him on the right day.[2]

Ludwig van Beethoven was born on December 16, 1770 in Bonn, in a little house on *Bonngasse*. His family soon moved to a bigger house on *Rheingasse* not far away.[3] Beethoven's grandfather had been *Kapellmeister* to the elector of Bonn and also a prosperous wine merchant. His father was merely a mediocre musician and, I'm sorry to say, a drunk.[4] Beethoven's father very much wanted the boy to become a musical prodigy, just like Mozart. Little Beethoven started piano lessons when he was very young, in fact so small that he had to stand on the piano bench to reach the keys. His father also told everyone that he was two years younger, just to make him seem more talented.[5]

Beethoven was a grubby little boy, the type who always forgets to wash behind his ears. He quit school at 11 and by 16 was court organist to the elector. He was already beginning to compose small pieces and was an absolute whiz at sight reading.[6]

In 1792 he moved to Vienna, where for a short while he took lessons from Haydn, Albrechtsberger and Salieri. He was

[1]Bach had an enormous brood of children, but that's something else entirely.
[2]He liked bad puns and pranks. He was sometimes a chair-puller.
[3]For years, tourists flocked to the *Rheingasse* house, took snapshots and told everybody that they'd seen Beethoven's birthplace. They hadn't.
[4]If he couldn't continue the family wine business, the least he could do was support it.
[5]Even Beethoven himself long thought he had been born in 1772.
[6]His court uniform was "a sea-green frock coat, green knee-breeches with buckles, stockings of white or black silk, shoes with black bow knots."

too pig-headed to learn much from any of them. Johann Schenk corrected Beethoven's exercises before he submitted them to Haydn, which saved him some embarrassment.

Beethoven was quite a hit in Viennese society as a concert pianist, even though he didn't have the proper sort of manner. The aristocracy expected him to be subservient and to know his place. Beethoven knew his place — it just wasn't the same place they expected of him. He once told off his patron, Prince Lichnowsky, with the remark: "There are and there will be thousands of princes. There is only one Beethoven."[7] He could be very stubborn when he wanted to be, which was most of the time. If he didn't feel like it, he wouldn't play when you asked him, even if, like the Countess Thun, you got down on your knees and begged him.[8]

He was too busy thinking about sublime music to worry himself about social niceties. Once when the violinist Ignaz Schuppanzigh complained about a particularly difficult passage in one of Beethoven's string quartets, the composer shouted at him: "I can't think about your miserable violin when I am speaking to my God." He had a raucous laugh and was inclined to spit whenever he felt the urge.

As you might expect with such a hot temper, Beethoven had real trouble keeping servants. They just wouldn't put up with him.[9] He didn't get along very well with landlords, either, so he had to move every few months.[10] He was a slob, basically. The Baron de Tremont swears that, on one visit, there was a full chamberpot under Beethoven's piano. When Beethoven came visiting, it was a good idea to hide away the fine porcelain. He dropped things.[11]

Beethoven was no better in restaurants. He would leave without paying the bill, or sometimes absent-mindedly pay for a meal he hadn't ordered. He scribbled music on the napkins,

[7]He had a point there.
[8]"But then," Frau von Bernhard reminds us, "Countess Thun was a very eccentric woman."
[9]In 1820, for instance, the kitchen maid he hired on April 17 he fired on May 16. The maid he hired on July 1 ran away on the 28th.
[10]One landlord in Baden was glad to have Beethoven as a tenant. After he left, the landlord auctioned off the window shutters, which were covered with musical notations.
[11]And he usually cut himself shaving.

tablecloths and menus. He once got so angry at a waiter that he dumped his plate of veal and gravy over the man's head.[12]

He was fond of fish, but his favorite dishes were scrambled eggs in a bread soup or a heaping bowl of macaroni and Parmesan cheese. He liked his coffee strong, always 60 beans to the cup.[13]

But we mustn't lose sight of what makes Beethoven important. He may have been a boor and a slob, but he was a great composer.[14] He wrote nine symphonies;[15] five piano concertos; 16 string quartets; 10 sonatas for violin and five for cello; 30 piano sonatas; two masses; more chamber music than I can name and a duet for obbligato eyeglasses.[16] He wrote one opera, *Fidelio*, and four overtures to start it off. The first three were trial runs and are now called the *Leonore Overtures*, just to avoid confusion. We know he was a great composer because his brain was so big. And, as Wagner pointed out, because it was encased in such a thick skull.[17]

Beethoven never married, although he liked to flirt, and his friend Wegler tells us that he was always in love with someone.[18] Perhaps, unlike Bach, Grieg or Stravinsky, he had no eligible cousins to marry. He proposed to Magdalene Willman, a singer in the Vienna court opera, but she refused him because "he was so ugly and half-cracked." It's probably just as well: Beethoven had syphilis.[19]

He was hardly the tall, dark, and handsome type. Well, he was dark, anyway. He had good teeth, piercing eyes and a stern,

---

[12]Then he burst out laughing. You could never tell with Beethoven.

[13]He was very careful to count them: never 59 or 61.

[14]The issue of greatness is sometimes problematical. Alfred Einstein, in his book *Greatness In Music*, gets at the heart of the matter when he asks: "Was Frederick the Great great?" Well, was he?

[15]Methodically numbered One through Nine.

[16]I'm not sure if those are alto eyeglasses in G or the baritone ones in C.

[17]As the autopsy report so eloquently puts it, his brain "contained a smaller proportion of water than is normal. The convolutions seemed to be of double depth and more numerous than ordinarily." *Something* must have been going on in there.

[18]He once boasted that, of all these infatuations, the longest lasted only seven months.

[19]Not to mention chronic constipation alternating with diarrhea, typhus and dropsy.

pocked-marked face. He was only five feet, four inches tall.[20]

After his brother Kasper died, Beethoven fought a long court battle with his sister-in-law Johanna for custody of her son Karl, Beethoven's nephew. Beethoven might have meant well for the boy, but he certainly had some nasty things to say about Johanna, whom he thought an unfit mother.[21] The years of the court battle took their toll on Beethoven, and it was all he could do to compose two cello concertos, three piano sonatas (including the *Hammerklavier* sonata) and the song cycle *An die ferne Geliebte*. Hardly worth mentioning, really.

Towering geniuses.

The biggest tragedy of Beethoven's life, of course, was his increasing deafness. He began to notice it when he was about 30 and before he was 50 he had lost his hearing entirely. As the years wore on, he broke more and more strings on his piano, pounding the keys trying to hear the sounds.

In the end, he fell apart completely and died in 1827. Anselm Hüttenbrenner, who was at his bedside, tells us that in his final moments, Beethoven roused himself from his coma to shake an angry fist at the heavens. There was a dramatic clap of thunder and a flash of lightning, and the great composer was dead.[22]

---

[20]Ranking him right up there with Mozart at 5' 4", Schubert at 5' 2", Wagner at 5' 5", Schoenberg at 5' 4", and Stravinsky at 5' 3". That's what you call "towering genius."

[21]When he was being polite, he called her "The Queen of the Night." I won't repeat what else he called her.

[22]We shouldn't trust Hüttenbrenner's word completely. After all, he was the one who lost the last two movements of Schubert's *Unfinished Symphony*.

At Beethoven's funeral, a crowd of 20,000 lined the streets to pay their last respects. Schubert and Hummel were among the pallbearers.[23]

Music history tends to romanticize Beethoven, seeing him as the mighty genius struggling against tragic deafness. I prefer to think of him in those moments when he took time out from composing glorious music to insult an aristocrat or dump dinner over a waiter's head.

[23]Luigi Lablache, an operatic bass who sang at the funeral, had also sung at Haydn's funeral. Later, he sang at Chopin's. He would have towered over Beethoven. He was nearly seven feet tall.

WAGNER

EITHER YOU LIKE WAGNER'S music or you don't. For some people, Wagnerian opera represents the highest form of art as a synthesis of music and drama. For others, it's just fat people shouting at each other in German for what seems like eternity. Personally, I'm inclined to agree with Rossini, who said that "Wagner has good moments, but bad quarter-hours."[1]

Wagner was born in 1813 in Leipzig to Johanna and her husband Carl Fredrich Wagner. The baby was named Wilhelm Richard, although he quickly dropped the Wilhelm.[2] Six months after the boy was born, Joanna's first husband died and she remarried an actor named Ludwig Geyer.[3] For a while in his boyhood, Richard took to using the surname Geyer, but he later changed it back to Wagner.[4]

As a boy, Wagner could be troublesome at times. Every few nights he would wake up screaming at the top of his lungs, just to let everyone know he was still there.[5] He didn't care for school much and was always playing hookey. One day, his school informed his parents that he hadn't been to classes in six months, and would they please tell him, if they saw him, that he shouldn't expect to graduate.

Wagner at this time had his heart set on becoming a famous poet or playwright. His first play, called *Leubald* and written when he was 14 or so, gave him some difficulty, since by the fourth act 42 characters have died. In order to make the plot work out, he

---

[1] That about sums it up.
[2] For reasons best understood by his parents, his boyhood nickname was "Cossack."
[3] Ludwig was what you might call a longtime friend of the family. Oddly enough, young Richard looked a lot like him.
[4] He thought it had a better ring to it.
[5] The singers in his operas do this, too.

had to bring back most of them as ghosts. Wagner showed this early work to hardly anyone, except his sister Cäcilie.[6]

When he was 15 years old, Wagner heard Beethoven's *Ninth Symphony* for the first time, and it had a profound effect on him.[7] From then on he decided to become a great composer just like Beethoven.[8]

Among Wagner's first compositions was a concert overture. To keep all the instruments apart in his own mind, he wrote the score in different colors: the strings were in red ink, the wood-winds in green, and the brass and percussion in black. The first performance was a disaster, since everyone in the audience snickered at the kettledrum.[9]

Wagner wrote the score in different colors.

Wagner enrolled at the University of Leipzig, where he majored in drinking and gambling, with a minor concentration to challenging others to sword duels.[10] He once gambled away his mother's entire pension, but luckily won it back again on an all-or-nothing wager. Wagner didn't stay long at university: he left when he found out they expected him to go to classes, too.

Despite the disaster of his overture and the fact that he did not perform very well on any instrument (he was a rotten pianist and sang badly), Wagner got a job directing a small

---

[6]Or was it Ottilie? Anyway, she said she liked it.
[7]Actually, it made him sick to his stomach, but he took that as a good sign.
[8]Wagner was convinced that Beethoven was the greatest musical genius ever born because Beethoven had such a thick skull. Well, *he* thought that was logical.
[9]Wagner's progress was severely hampered when he nearly ran out of green ink.
[10]Which he never fought.

opera company in Magdeburg, where he met and married one of the singers, Minna Planer.

The first performance of a Wagner opera took place in Magdeburg in 1836. *Das Liebesverbot*, based on Shakespeare's *Measure For Measure*, was not a rousing success: there were barely two performances. On the first night, the leading tenor forgot most of his lines and hid behind a big feather boa, hoping that might help.[11] The second night never really got off the ground at all. The leading soprano's jealous husband went backstage and punched the second tenor on the nose, thinking they were having an affair. When she tried to stop her husband, he hit her too, and she fainted.

To make matters worse, Wagner's pet dog, a poodle, had run away from home.[12]

In view of his operatic failure and to avoid paying the increasing debts, Wagner and Minna resorted to a strategy they were to follow many times again: they left town in a hurry. Hoping to put as much distance as possible between themselves and their angry creditors, the Wagners sailed to France and settled in Paris, where Wagner earned money doing hack work for a music publisher. Some musicologists think that the boat voyage to France helped inspire Wagner to compose his opera *Der Fliegende Holländer*, or the Flying Dutchman.[13]

Dutchman and an earlier opera, *Rienzi*, were received favorably, so Wagner was offered a job as second *Kapellmeister* to the Dresden opera house. He had to promise not to tamper with the way they performed Mozart and other standards.

Wagner set to work on two more operas, *Tannhäuser* and *Lohengrin*. The first performance of *Tannhäuser* in 1845 went well, but left the audience rather bewildered.[14] But he was just warming up. The real confusion would soon follow.

Wagner got caught up in a revolutionary movement for a while and wrote angry tracts denouncing capitalism.[15] But when the revolution was suppressed, he fled to Weimer and the pro-

---

[11]It never does.

[12]Wagner had dogs all his life. Over the years there were two black poodles, Speck and Dreck; several Newfoundlands; two spaniels, Peps and Fips; a few terriers; and a Spitz named Putzi.

[13]Or maybe it just made him seasick.

[14]It's much the same today.

[15]Maybe he thought it was a way to wipe out his debts.

tection of the pianist and composer Franz Liszt.[16] Wagner's socialist phase didn't last very long, and within a few years he was writing about "the vulgar egotism of the masses."

Apart from his music, Wagner wrote essays and diatribes on a whole range of subjects, most of which he knew nothing about. There was that bit about Beethoven's skull and also some unforgivably libelous insults flung at Jews.[17] In his later years, Wagner began extolling the virtues of vegetarianism. If we all stopped eating meat and ate only vegetables and fruit, he said, the world would be a better place.[18] The lake shores in the North of Canada, Wagner wrote, are crowded with vegetarian panthers and tigers.[19]

But Wagner's essays are nothing compared to his contribution to the development of opera. Having decided out of the blue that all great art must take its inspiration from pre-Christian mythology, Wagner set out to create an epic saga combining music and drama in one unified art work, which he called *Gesamtkunstwerk*.[20]

Wagner's theories saw their fulfilment in his opera cycle *Der Ring des Nibelungen*, which is actually made up of four operas.[21] He took a break in the middle to compose *Tristan und Isolde*, but that's hardly worth mentioning. Together, the four operas of the Ring cycle tell the story of a magic ring that everyone is fighting over. It is guarded by the Rhine maidens and stolen by the dwarf Alberich. In fact, nearly everybody makes a try to steal the ring: Fafnir, the giant who looks like a dragon; Wotan, the ruler of the gods; Mime, another dwarf; and Siegfried, the dashing hero.

Siegfried's parentage, not unlike Wagner's himself, is rather complicated, since his mother and father, Sieglinde and Siegmund, were actually twin brother and sister.[22] The whole

---

[16]Not to mention his daughter Cosima. More on her later.
[17]Adolf Hitler thought Wagner was wonderful. Does that give you the idea?
[18]He also thought that we should all move to the equatorial zones, where this would be easier.
[19]If there were any vegetarian panthers and tigers in Canada in the late 19th century, they're gone by now.
[20]Sounds a little bit like a sneeze, doesn't it?
[21]Just for the record, they are *Das Rheingold*, *Die Walküre*, *Siegfried*, and *Götterdämmerung*.
[22]Where's the League of Moral Decency when you really need it?

story gets even more complicated, what with Brünhilde and the rest. But I'd rather not go into it. Altogether, the Ring operas take about 22 hours to perform.[23]

As part of his theory of *Gesamtkunstwerk*, Wagner developed a compositional style he called "endless melody."[24] To do this, he created a *leitmotiv*, or little tune, to represent each important character and many of the stage props in the play. There's one for Siegfried, one for the ring, one for his sword and so on — 90 of them in all.[25] The *leitmotivs* help the audience to figure out what's happening on stage, which is particularly useful if you've bought a cheap seat way in the back of the hall and can't see what's going on. Claude Debussy thought the *leitmotivs* were silly, saying: "The *leitmotiv* system suggests a world of harmless lunatics who present their visiting cards and shout their name in song."

Speaking of harmless lunatics, Wagner got most of the money to build his enormous opera house in Bayreuth from the Mad King Ludwig of Bavaria. Ludwig was called Mad for a variety of reasons, only one of which was for giving so much money to Wagner.[26]

Wagner's attitude to marriage was, shall we say, less than exemplary. There always seemed to be some woman whom he found more interesting, for a while at least, than his wife, Minna. Over the years, he spent an evening or several with Mathilde Wesendonk (whose husband, Otto, gave Wagner money anyway to help finance opera productions), Julie Schwabe, Judith Gautier,[27] and of course, Cosima Liszt.[28] He tells about most of these women (and others) in his autobiography, *Mein Leben*, which he dictated to Cosima.[29]

She makes an interesting study herself: Cosima was illegitimate, too, the middle of three children born to Liszt and Marie

---

[23]Wagner's total output was about 61 hours of music in 53 years of composing, or a little better than one hour per year. It's not so bad when you look at it that way.

[24]It certainly seems that way when you're listening to it.

[25]Wagner would feel right at home composing for television shows.

[26]Ludwig's private life was the sort on which gossip flourished.

[27]When he was 63 and she was 24 he tried to impress her by climbing a tree. It must have worked.

[28]Oh yes, and her older sister, Blandine.

[29]And I'll bet he didn't even blush.

d'Agoult, who later went on to write novels under the name Daniel Stern.[30] Cosima, whose nickname was "Stork," married Hans von Bülow, himself an accomplished pianist and conductor. Von Bülow became a great champion of Wagner's music, even after he found out that the composer and his wife had become, well, rather friendly.[31] Wagner and Cosima had two more children, Eva and Siegfried. They even got married for the last one. Von Bülow had got fed up with it all after the second child and began to turn his attention to the music of Brahms, who was a bachelor.[32]

Wagner definitely let success go to his head, and in the years before his death in 1883 he indulged himself fully in his love of luxury. Most of his final opera, *Parsifal*, was composed after hours of soaking in a hot tub full of perfume. His demands for fine clothing made from satin, silk and fur trim taxed the resources of his seamstress.[33] He was particularly fond of a "pale and delicate" shade of pink."[34]

"Mine is a highly susceptible, intense, voracious sensuality," he wrote, "which must somehow or other be indulged if my mind is to accomplish the agonizing labor of calling a non-existent world into being."

Fair enough. After all, what's a few pairs of pink silk underwear if it means all 22 hours of the Ring Cycle? Do you really want me to answer that?[35]

But let's give the last word to Friedrich Nietzsche. "Is Wagner a human being at all? Is he not rather a disease?" Good question.

[30]When Cosima was born, Marie was still married to Count Charles d'Agoult, but that was a mere technicality. The count wasn't very sure of paternity most of the time, either. He solved the problem by referring to all of them as "my wife's children."
[31]The baby was born in 1865 and they named her Isolde. Isn't that cute?
[32]Brahms was probably having an affair with Robert Schumann's widow, Clara. But let's not get into that.
[33]Her name was Bertha.
[34]Freud would have had a field day with Wagner, but this was before Freud really got started.
[35]One French reviewer called Wagner's operas "the music of a demented eunuch."

BRAHMS

EVERYONE KNOWS BRAHMS: he wrote that lullaby. But let's be fair, there was more to him than that. He also wrote a *Requiem*.[1] If you want to impress your friends, you could refer to his famous lullaby as the *Wiengenlied*, Opus 49 No. 4. If you have friends who are impressed by that sort of thing, you're welcome to them.[2]

Johannes Brahms was born in 1833 in Hamburg, where his parents were living at the time.[3] His father, Jakob, was a double-bass player, though not very good at it. His mother, Christine, was a seamstress. She was 41 when she married Jakob, and 17 years older than he was. It was an odd match. Young Johannes got his early musical training from his father, although his mother may have contributed to his ability to weave complicated melodic lines into the fabric of his music.[4]

Money was always scarce when Brahms was growing up, and even as a young boy he supplemented the family income by playing the piano in some of the seedy bars and taverns in the dockyards. He didn't enjoy it very much, but it was a living.[5]

Although most of us picture Brahms as he was in later life — sloppy looking, with a bushy white beard, long grey hair, and baggy clothing — the truth is he was once a slim, blue-eyed blond and considered quite handsome. It shows what can happen when you smoke too many cheap cigars.[6]

[1]Well, all right. He wrote some symphonies, too.
[2]As you might expect, Brahms composed his Opus 49 not long after he had finished Opus 48, and just before beginning Opus 50. He had an orderly mind.
[3]It was easier that way.
[4]She also had a limp, which might explain his love of cross rhythms.
[5]He later performed in places with a better class of clientele.
[6]His eyes remained blue throughout his life, but the rest of him went all to pieces.

Brahms never married, although he came close once. All those years playing piano in sailors' bordellos had made a deep impression on his young mind: I'm afraid it gave him a rather scornful attitude towards women. According to some sources, much of his trouble came from the fact that his voice did not break until he was 24 years old.[7]

The woman he almost married was a singer named Agathe. They became unofficially engaged, but Brahms backed out at the last minute, telling her in a panic: "I love you but I cannot wear fetters."[8]

In later life he even began to resemble a hedgehog.

Although Brahms was born in Hamburg and worked for a time in Leipzig, he spent most of his life in Vienna.[9] He lived the last 26 years of his life in the same apartment. Either he liked it or he was too lazy to move. He usually dined in his favorite pub, The Red Hedgehog.[10]

[7]Four years later, at 28, he finally put away his favorite tin soldiers. I don't know what became of them. There's probably a PhD thesis in there somewhere.
[8]This remark caused her more grief than it needed to: She may have thought he'd said "feathers."
[9]He sometimes spent holidays in Baden-Baden.
[10]In later life he even began to resemble a hedgehog.

It was in Vienna that the young Brahms met Robert Schumann and his wife, Clara. By this time, Schumann was beginning to hear strange noises. In one of his few lucid moments he wrote an enthusiastic essay for his old music journal about how wonderful Brahms's music was. Brahms meanwhile was falling in love with Schumann's wife.[11]

Many composers in his own day were inclined to dismiss Brahms as unimportant, since he always stayed with the old-fashioned classical forms and didn't explore new compositional techniques the way, say, Wagner did. Brahms felt that if it was good enough for Beethoven it was good enough for him. But the Wagnerites thought that he should expand his horizons. What his symphonies need, they would say, are a few robust Wagner Tubas.[12] In my books, Brahms is one of the greatest composers who ever lived, since he wrote no operas. Anyone who avoids operas can't be all bad.

It was conductor Hans von Bülow who included Brahms as one of "The three B's," along with Bach and Beethoven.[13] Nowadays this seems quite sensible, but in Brahms's time the remark caused quite a commotion. No one agrees on who should be considered the fourth B, if there is one."[14]

[11]Personally, I think more has been made of this than the facts warrant. But you know how people will talk.

[12]The Wagner Tuba, oddly enough, was invented by Wagner. Some people can never get enough of them.

[13]Von Bülow also referred to Brahms's *First Symphony* as "Beethoven's Tenth." He was a great one for a catchy phrase.

[14]Have you ever noticed how many famous composers have names beginning with B? There's Binchois, Byrd, Buxetehude, Bach, Benda, Boccherini, Beethoven, Balakirev, Borodin, Berlioz, Bruckner, Bizet, Bartok, Britten, Berg, Bernstein, Berio, Boulez, and of course Samuel Barber. I find this enormously inspiring.

FOLLOW THE LIEDER

SCHUBERT

FOR SOME REASON, MANY PEOPLE have trouble telling Schubert and Schumann apart. It's really quite simple: Schubert was the short, dumpy one, with curly black hair and little wire-rimmed glasses. Schumann was taller and married to Clara.

But telling their music apart is a whole different story, one that takes years of study. Both composers lived in the first half of the 19th century and wrote *lieder*, which is the plural of *lied*, which is German for song.[1] These were written for a singer and piano accompaniment. Most of them are love songs about roses and mill streams and other pretty things. But some of them are about nasty spirits in the woods and broken hearts and other aspects of life that I'd rather not think about.

Franz Peter Schubert was born in 1797 in Vienna, in a little neighborhood called *Himmelpfortgrund*, the 12th of 14 children.[2] His father was a schoolteacher, and ran the school privately out of his home. As a small boy, Schubert sang at the Royal Seminary, where he was allowed to wear a spiffy uniform that included a three-cornered hat.[3]

Little Franz was quite the musical prodigy, and at age 11 began taking lessons in theory and composition from Antonio Salieri.[4] When he was older, he taught for a while in his father's school, but after four years he couldn't stand a room full of

---

[1]Don't ask me why the plural of *lied* is *lieder* and not *lieds*. German is just like that.

[2]His oldest brother, Ignaz, was born just two months after their parents were married. It rarely came up in the conversation.

[3]If Schubert had really been on top of things, he might have thought to write a ballet about his three-cornered hat. But that had to wait until 1919 and Manuel de Falla.

[4]Oh, you remember: he's the one who didn't actually poison Mozart.

screaming ankle-biters any longer. He quit teaching and took to living the life of a bohemian composer. He got rather good at it, in fact.

In the mornings, if he didn't have too much of a hangover, he would compose songs, chamber music, symphonies, and operas with bad librettos. In the afternoons, he would hang around the cafés of Vienna, eating *Sachertorte* and talking with his friends. These were mostly other musicians and poets, and a scruffy bunch all around. Evenings were the time for drinking and more talk about the importance of the arts in the general scheme of things. The next morning he would do it all again. It was a simple life, and it suited Schubert to the ground. Naturally, he was always short of cash. His friends called him *Schwammerl*, or "Tubby."[5]

His friends called him "Little Mushroom."

As with all artists throughout the ages, Schubert felt that what he was doing was terribly, terribly important. "The state should keep me," he once told someone. "I have come into the world for no purpose but to compose."[6]

Every once in a while, he would make a half-hearted attempt to get a job playing the piano for an opera company or some-

---

[5]It's actually German for "little mushroom."
[6]A lot of others have felt the same way. It never seems to work out.

thing. The jobs never lasted very long. For one thing, punctuality was not his strong point.

Schubert never married. Probably too busy. He did have a roving eye, but he was very shy. His first true love was a woman named Therese Grob. She married a baker. Schubert taught piano for a while to the two daughters of a Hungarian nobleman. He thought the older one was cute and he enjoyed flirting with the nobleman's maid, whose name was Pepi Pöckelhofer.[7]

Schubert was not terribly well known in his own lifetime, although his friends would get together now and then for an evening concert entirely devoted to his music. These concerts were called "Schubertiads."[8] He gave only one public concert in his life, which the newspapers hardly mentioned, being all agog with the recent appearance in Vienna of the violin virtuoso Niccolo Paganini. He was considered more interesting because he had sold his soul to the devil.

Schubert didn't have much luck with publishers, either. When he sent a copy of his song *Die Erlkönig* to one publisher, the editors sent it back to the only Franz Schubert they knew, a third-rate composer in Dresden. The other Schubert replied with a nasty letter, saying he didn't want to be bothered with such "wretched stuff." Few of Schubert's compositions were published in his own lifetime and those that were did not sell very well.[9]

Considering the brief span of Schubert's life — he died at 31 in 1828 — he churned out a remarkable amount of music: nine symphonies,[10] 19 string quartets, 10 operas, a whole bunch of piano sonatas, chamber music of all kinds, and more than 600 songs. He was probably the only one who could match Mozart for speed.[11] For some reason, the overture he wrote for his opera *Die Zauberharfe* is now known as the overture to *Rosamunde*,

---

[7]Somewhere along the line he got syphilis, but I'm not sure from whom. All his hair fell out, but it grew back eventually.

[8]Or, if you prefer the German, *Schubertiaden*.

[9]A piano tutor by Johann Nepomuk Hummel sold 1,800 copies on the first day it was published. People knew what they liked.

[10]He matched Beethoven but couldn't beat him.

[11]Schumann said that Schubert's melodies are full of "compressed, lyrical insanity." Improve on that, would you?

which is another piece entirely. Don't bother trying to figure that out: it makes no sense.

Ironically, one of his most famous works is a symphony that he never finished.[12] No one really knows why he never finished it, although there are a lot of theories.

Some think that Schubert would have finished it if he'd had time. On the other hand, maybe he just ran out of ideas.

In his final illness, the bedridden Schubert read widely, and grew fond of the Leatherstocking novels of James Fenimore Cooper. *The Last Of The Mohicans* was a particular favorite.

Schumann discovered the manuscript of Schubert's *Ninth Symphony* at Schubert's brother's house, sitting in a pile of papers at the piano. He never was very tidy.

[12]This is harder than you might imagine. Otherwise there would be many more composers more famous than they are.

SCHUMANN

ROBERT SCHUMANN WAS NOT nearly as interesting as Schubert, although he had his moments. When he wasn't rooting around Schubert's papers, looking for lost symphonies, he was busy composing his own music.

He was born in 1810 in Zwickau. His father was a bookseller, and instilled in him a lifelong passion for literature. After an unremarkable childhood, he went to Leipzig as a young man to study law. That was the idea, although he spent most of his time going to concerts, practising the piano and smoking cigars. He liked beer, too.

At 20, Schumann began studying piano under Friedrich Wieck, whose 11-year-old daughter, Clara, was already a formidable concert pianist, and the cutest little girl you ever saw. Schumann moved into the Wieck home to be closer to his teacher.[1]

Schumann made a promising start, and Wieck thought he had great talent. But his future as a concert pianist came to a sorry end when, in an effort to strengthen the fingers of his right hand, he invented a harness contraption that permanently crippled two of his fingers. It also made his handwriting a mess.[2] Well, it seemed like a good idea at the time.[3]

Schumann was also extremely nearsighted and afraid of heights, as his exemption from military service notes. He lived in ground-floor apartments whenever possible.

[1] Would *you* want to live in the same house as your piano teacher? I know I wouldn't.
[2] Scholars disagree over which fingers were affected. I say let them argue. It provides useful fodder for learned music journals.
[3] One remedy prescribed by the best doctors was for Schumann to soak his injured hand in the guts of a freshly slaughtered animal. They don't specify what sort of animal.

Schumann didn't fall in love with Clara Wieck right away. After all, she was still too young. He was rather smitten with another of Wieck's pupils, one Ernestine von Fricken.[4] She was plumpish and pleasant — though not, we're told, an intellectual wonder. His enthusiasm for her seems to have waned when he discovered that she was not a baron's daughter after all, but only the illegitimate daughter of the baron's unmarried sister-in-law. Hard luck.

Schumann's finger strengthener.

The various movements of his piano piece *Carnaval* are based on a musical theme derived from the name of the town where Ernestine's family lived.[5]

Schumann was always doing things like that: deriving clever musical themes from words.[6] His first published pieces, the *ABEGG Variations*, were written for the daughter of a Mannheim family named, of course, Abegg. The music was published in 1830 by Friedrich Kistner, "a publisher," Schumann notes in his diary, "whom I declare for the benefit of posterity and all other composers to be a rogue." Sounds like they had a typical composer/publisher relationship.

By this time, Schumann and Clara had decided that they were madly in love and meant for each other. They began writ-

[4]Of the Bohemian von Frickens.
[5]Opinion on *Carnaval* was divided: Liszt thought it among the greatest works ever written. Chopin, on the other hand, thought it was barely music.
[6]The Medieval term for this device is *soggetto cavato*, in case you were wondering.

ing letters back and forth like nobody's business. Clara's father objected strenuously, calling Schumann a no-good and a drunkard, and generally trying to discourage the match.[7] He should have known that children are not like that: the more you tell them not to do something, the more they want to do it. In November of 1835, Schumann kissed Clara for the first time. He wrote it down in his diary so he wouldn't forget. She was 16 and he was 25.

Wieck still objected to their relationship, but the lovers hung in there. Eventually they took the matter to court and the judge allowed the marriage in 1849. They were very happy and had eight children.[8]

Although successful both as a composer and a critic, Schumann's talents as a conductor were minimal. He usually just waved his arms about in a bit of a daze.[9] On one memorable occasion, he continued to beat time after the music had stopped. This is considered bad form.

As a composer, he is best remembered for his piano works, such as *Carnaval*, *Papillons*, and the A-minor piano concerto. He wrote more than 250 songs. In later life he wrote four symphonies and a failed opera.

Schumann was a music critic for many years and established his own music journal, of which he was editor. This is as neat a way as any of assuring that your writing gets published. He wrote under two pen names, either Florestan or Eusebius. As Florestan he was gushy and over-enthusiastic; as Eusebius he was more level-headed. His most famous remark as a critic was his first impression of the music of Frederick Chopin, of which (as Florestan) he said: "Hats off, gentlemen, a genius!" That does have a nice ring to it, the sort of remark that nowadays Chopin would put on his first album cover.

Schumann seems to have had some difficulty distinguishing between fantasy and reality with this literary device: two of the movements of *Carnaval* are dedicated to Florestan and Eusebius.

---

[7]There's a whole theory here that Schumann had syphilis, which accounted for the injured hand, among other things. I'm choosing to ignore it, as it only complicates matters needlessly.
[8]Oh, sure they bickered now and then. Who doesn't?
[9]This may sound just like most conductors you've ever seen. But there's supposed to be more to it than that.

In fact, towards the end Schumann had real trouble with reality most of the time. He heard strange voices and other noises: he also said that the spirits of Schubert and Mendelssohn came to him to dictate musical themes. Sometimes he thought he was being pursued by tigers and hyenas.[10]

After attempting suicide in the Rhine, he was voluntarily committed to an asylum, where he lived out his remaining few years, dying in 1856. He was often troubled by the sound of a continuous A ringing in his ears.[11]

Still, you have to admit that he wrote some fine music. So what if he was a little bonkers sometimes? We must tolerate a bit of craziness: it fuels the creative spirit.

[10]Maybe he was. Who knows?
[11]Bedrich Smetana wrote that in the final years of his deafness he often heard the sound of a first-inversion A-flat major triad in a very high register. This happened each evening between six and seven p.m., regular as clockwork.

THE RUSSIANS
ARE COMING,
THE RUSSIANS
ARE COMING.

THE MIGHTY FIVE

THE RUSSIANS WERE INTRODUCED to Western music in the 10th century, when Prince Vladimir of Kiev decided that everybody should become Christian.[1] Before then, the Russians had only been interested in singing their own folk songs. Once the Church got established, it didn't think much of folk music at all. Church authorities thought it was a distraction.

The Mighty Five

Things finally came to a head in 1636, when the leader of the Church, the patriarch Joseph, banned all music-making in the home. In Moscow, 50 wagon-loads of instruments were burned in a big bonfire and dumped into the river. All the peasants thought it was a party: they stood around and cheered. I

[1]He'd heard reports of church ceremonies in Byzantium, and he was particularly impressed by all the smells and bells.

don't think they understood whose instruments they were. Those things cost money, you know.

A little while later, Peter the Great said music wasn't so bad after all, and formed a military band just to get things going again. His daughter, the Empress Elizabeth, liked opera, although her servants had to go door to door to convince the other nobles to come to the theatre. By the time of Catherine the Great they didn't need convincing any more. Catherine was particularly fond of comic French opera.[2]

Mikhail Glinka is the first Russian composer worth any mention: everyone before him had been a trial model. Glinka decided that what he needed to do was establish a truly Russian style of music. None of this imported variety for him. He realized that what the Russians did better than nearly anyone else was to sing folk songs, so he based much of his music on those. This time no one set fire to him or dumped him into the river.

Glinka is best remembered for two operas: *A Life For The Tsar* and *Russlan And Ludmilla*. Neither of them was particularly well received at its premiere performance. *A Life For The Tsar* got a tepid reaction at best. Maybe part of the problem was that Glinka wrote the overture first and then the opera to follow it. You can't get ahead that way.[3]

Russlan fared even worse. At the first performance, even some of the singers and members of the orchestra booed the production.[4]

Glinka was a weakling child and a lazy adult. He was weepy, romantic and fell in love every few weeks or so. But he is considered the father of Russian music, so what can I say?

The composer who really brought Russian music into its own was Mily Balakirev, who was born in 1837 in the little village of Nijni-Novgorod. He was stocky, with a big square head, thick neck, and squinty little eyes. He worked most of his life for the government.[5]

Balakirev gathered around him a group of four other young composers, who all believed that Russian music was the greatest thing since sliced bread. They were César Cui, Alexander

[2]Anything else was more than her brain could cope with.
[3]It's just not done in the best circles.
[4]Constantine Bachturin had been drunk when he wrote the plot outline, which probably didn't help matters.
[5]Does that give you the idea?

110

Borodin, Nicolai Rimsky-Korsakov, and Modest Mussorgsky. The five of them would gather at Balakirev's home and talk about music till all hours of the morning. Together they have come to be known as The Mighty Five, or The Mighty Handful. In France they're called *Les Cinq*.[6] Their nickname comes from the Russian *Moguchaya Kuchka*, or "The Mighty Little Heap." (A heap of what I don't know.)

The Mighty Five were all for Russian music and they didn't mind saying so. If you weren't, you were no friend of theirs. They had some pretty angry things to say about Tchaikovsky and Anton Rubenstein, who didn't sound Russian enough to suit them.[7]

Cui was the son of a soldier in Napoleon's army who stayed behind in Russia after his comrades had left. His father had three sons, whom he named César, Alexander and Napoleon, so a military career seemed inevitable for all of them. Cui grew up poor and remained thrifty, not to say downright stingy, all of his life. His idea of a real splurge was to have tea with jam.

Although he was a composer with the rest, his greater role was as a journalist, championing the music of Russian nationalism that his fiends were writing.(Cui's opera *Ratcliff* had seven decent performances in 1869, but the eighth was so bad that Cui himself panned it in the paper the next day.) Cui eventually rose to the rank of general in the Russian army. He lived to the ripe old age of 83 and taught military strategy and fortifications right up to the end. If you ask how to pronounce his name I can't help you. You're on your own.

Mussorgsky came from a wealthy noble family and could trace his roots back 32 generations to the very first Russian dynasty. He always pronounced his name *Muss*orgsky, with the accent on the first syllable. Nobody ever listened to him, and today we all pronounce it Muss*or*gsky, which sounds right to us. He served for a while in the army as a lieutenant, and then got a cushy job at the ministry of transport.

Mussorgsky was always especially fond of his mother, so he took it rather hard when she died. He took to spending rather a lot of time with her best friend, an older woman. I'm not

[6]Not to be confused with *Les Six*.
[7]Balakirev once called Rubenstein an "idiot," and that's about as polite as he ever got.

entirely sure this relationship was very healthy: it was certainly the sort that gave people something to talk about. Mussorgsky's nickname was Modinka. Cui called him this all the time.

Mussorgsky's best-known composition is *Pictures At An Exhibition*. He wrote it for piano, not realizing that everyone would much rather listen to it played by full orchestra. He also wrote *Boris Godunov* and one other opera, and left two more unfinished when he died. This he did quite suddenly at the age of 41 after having far too much to drink.[8]

Rimsky-Korsakov was a Navy man and as a small boy once fell off the mast of a ship just to get used to the idea.[9] Balakirev brought him into the group when he was a young man and always considered him his favorite. While all the others were busy talking, Rimsky-Korsakov actually got down to the business of composing music. Unless you grew up on another planet, you will have heard his *Scheherazade* suite, and probably *Capriccio Espagnol*. His opera *Mozart and Salieri* is largely responsible for perpetuating the idea that Mozart was murdered by his jealous rival.[10] He wrote about 11 other operas, but their titles don't leap to mind.

Among his operas is one with the cumbersome title of *The Tale Of The Tsar Saltan, His Son The Famous And Mighty Prince Guidon Saltanovich, And The Beautiful Swan Princess*. He might have entered this in a contest for Longest Opera Title, but I can't be sure.[11] The only music anyone still know from this is a piece from the third act, which we now call *The Flight Of The Bumblebee*.

Borodin was born out of wedlock, but you hardly ever heard him mention it. His father, Prince Luka Gedeonoshvili, always said he meant to marry Borodin's mother, but somehow he forgot. Borodin grew up referring to himself as a girl and always called his mother "Auntie," but other than that he had a normal childhood. He tried to blow up the house a few times, since his mother had made the mistake of giving him a chemistry

---

[8]This had got to be a regular habit, I'm sorry to say.
[9]He tells us that the mast was seven storeys tall, but he might have exaggerated just a bit.
[10]There's probably not much truth to it, but it makes a good story, so who cares?
[11]I can't imagine it not winning if he did.

set.[12] He eventually became a doctor of medicine and a full-time professor of chemistry.[13] Music was just a hobby.

It cheers me up, and you may be glad to hear too, that Borodin was awkward as a young man dating girls. He once showed his date the linen closet, since he couldn't think of anything else.[14] Later, he got better at it, and had both a wife and a mistress. He wrote long letters to his wife, telling her how much he liked his mistress. She probably didn't want to hear about it.

Borodin's best-known composition is his opera *Prince Igor*, which Rimsky-Korsakov finished for him after he died. The *Polovtsian Dances* from Act II are still played today. He also wrote a whole set of variations on *Chopsticks*.[15]

As the years wore on, the members of The Mighty Five gradually drifted apart: somehow the magic had gone out of their relationship. Rimsky-Korsakov, Borodin and Balakirev all died of heart attacks. That's three out of five, or 60 per cent — rather a high average, I'd say. It comes from worrying so much about the future of Russian music.[16]

Poor old Balakirev came to the sorriest end. He became very superstitious and took to consulting a fortune teller almost daily. He stopped eating red meat, and would eat only fish that had "gone to sleep." Don't ask me how he could tell the difference.

[12]This is never a wise gift for a child.
[13]His *Researches on the Fluoride of Benzol* was a big hit in 1863.
[14]Her reaction has not been recorded. She probably said it was nice.
[15]*Chopsticks* was first published in Glasgow in 1877, in case you were wondering.
[16]Don't do this yourself. It's not worth it.

TCHAIKOVSKY

TCHAIKOVSKY WAS ONE OF THOSE weepy, emotional types. There was nothing he liked better than a good cry. If he couldn't cry, he would settle for a long whimper. It made him feel better.

Peter Ilyich was always a sensitive little boy. The slightest word of reproach from his nanny would send him scurrying off to the corner for a long sulk.[1] She called him "a porcelain child."[2] As he grew older, Tchaikovsky developed this into an art: he became a master pouter. His music is pretty weepy, too.

He began taking piano lessons at age seven after becoming fascinated with a small music box that played excerpts from Mozart's *Don Giovanni*. It was the beginning of his lifelong admiration for Mozart's music.[3]

Tchaikovsky studied law and for a while was employed as a legal clerk for the government. There, he perfected the art of looking busy while doing very little. He didn't begin to study music seriously until he was 21. He was a late bloomer, but he made up for it. He once confessed that before he began at the St. Petersburg Conservatory under Anton Rubenstein, he didn't even know how many symphonies Beethoven had composed.[4]

His first commissioned piece as a composer was written for the Russian prince and his Danish bride, a little overture on the Danish national anthem. They gave him a pair of jewelled cufflinks, which he promptly sold to a fellow student.[5]

[1]Her name was Fanny.
[2]She probably called him other things, too, even less complimentary. They have not been recorded.
[3]Mozart sounds better on a music box than most other composers.
[4]It was nine, remember?
[5]It was one of his brighter financial moves. Normally he just squandered his money.

Although he gained fame as a composer, Tchaikovsky never had what it takes to be a good conductor, even of his own music. He was always very nervous and had a morbid fear that his head might fall off in the middle of the piece. So he propped it up with his left hand and conducted only with his right.[6]

Tchaikovsky feared his head might fall off.

From 1872-76 he was a music critic for the *Moscow Gazette*, but we shouldn't hold that against him. He formed definite opinions about the work of other composers: he thought Wagner was boring, Bach only so-so and Handel fourth-rate. He also had some reservations about Beethoven. He liked Brahms as a person but hated his music.[7]

Tchaikovsky's love life was, to put it bluntly, confused. As a young man he thought he was in love with an operatic soprano named Desiree Artot, but he was wrong there. He even went so far as to marry a young woman named Antonina Miliukova.[8] He

[6]This does no good. How could he turn the pages?
[7]"Is Brahms deep?" he asks. Compared to what?
[8]"I shall make a serious effort to become legally married to somebody," he wrote to his brother Modest. It hardly sounds romantic.

shouldn't have bothered.[9] The marriage was a disaster from start to finish and lasted all of nine weeks. (That's scarcely enough time to unwrap the wedding presents.)

In a fit of depression, Tchaikovsky attempted suicide. He immersed himself in the River Neva, hoping to catch pneumonia. Wouldn't you know it, all he got was a terrible cold. After he left Antonina, she had a string of lovers and at least one child. When they met years later, they actually had a pleasant chat. She died in a mental asylum.

That same year, 1877, was a good one in another respect, though. Tchaikovsky got a fan letter from a woman named Nadedja von Meck, a 46-year-old widow with 11 children and more money than she knew what to do with.

She thought it would be rather fun to have a composer she could call her own. She agreed to send Tchaikovsky a regular allowance so that he could be free to spend his time composing. Her only rather eccentric stipulation was that they should never meet. They wrote letters back and forth all the time for 14 years but never met each other. (Actually, they did accidentally bump into each other once, on the road. But each of them hurried away, too embarrassed to say anything. So that doesn't count.)[10]

Tchaikovsky was a prolific composer who is best remembered now for his later symphonies and his ballet music (*Swan Lake, Sleeping Beauty*, and *The Nutcracker*).[11] He wrote chamber music and other orchestral pieces, including the famous B-flat-minor piano concerto.[12] He considered his *Symphony No. 6 (Pathetique)* to be his best work.

Only two of his eight operas ever really caught on, *Eugene Onegin* and *The Queen Of Spades*. *Vakula the Smith* was never a big hit, even after he changed the title to *The Shoes*.[13] Changing the title just wasn't going to be enough., His first opera, *The Opritchnik*, is all about the secret police of Ivan the Terrible. It's

[9]It went against his nature.

[10]As a young man, Claude Debussy taught piano to von Meck's daughter. He even asked to marry her, but mamma said he wasn't good enough for her.

[11]You thought I was going to forget the *1812 Overture*, didn't you? It's the one with the cannons.

[12]Which Rubenstein declared "unplayable" when he first saw it. He changed his mind when it became popular. Rubenstein wasn't one to miss a bandwagon when he saw one.

[13]Nor when he changed it again to *The Caprices of Oxana*.

not performed much any more. Secret police were a touchy subject in Soviet Russia, and even nowadays it's iffy.[14]

In recent years, it has become fashionable to spell Tchaikovsky's name Chaikovsky, or even Chaikovski. This is nothing more than a make-work project for librarians. I for one will have nothing to do with it.

Tchaikovsky died in 1893, a famous and successful man. No less an authority than the latest edition of Grove's dictionary says that he took poison rather than face the scandal of admitting to an affair with the young nephew of a prominent nobleman. Grove's says the story that he died of cholera from drinking unboiled water is pure hogwash. I'm not going to argue with the experts.

---

[14]He had abandoned work on an earlier opera, *Mandragora*. The libretto was just too silly.

A RIDICULOUSLY SHORT HISTORY OF OPERA

OPERA

....

THERE WILL ALWAYS BE PEOPLE who believe that opera represents the highest form of artistic achievement in music. They believe this because they think that everyone else believes it.[1] Opera is the plural in Latin for *opus*, which means "work," which is what it takes to listen to opera.[2]

It's all Monteverdi's fault, really. If he hadn't written that music drama *Orfeo* in 1607, this whole opera craze might never have started.[3] But having started, opera became all the rage. The Church in Rome did its best to suppress the development. The Church thought instead that composers should concentrate their energies on creating oratorios. This only worked some of the time.[4]

By the 17th and 18th centuries, operas had been divided into two distinct types: *opera seria* and *opera buffa*, or serious and comic opera. Operatic singers gained great popularity and enormous influence in both music and politics, and the most popular voice of this time in Italy was the *castrato*. Small boys with promising voices were often turned into *castrati* whether they wanted it or not.[5] In 18th-century Italy, about 4,000 boys met this fate, most of whom fell by the wayside.

Probably the best and the most famous of the *castrati* was Carlo Broschi, known as Farinelli. He could sing circles around

---

[1] Psychologists call this "mob mentality."

[2] Some people think the plural of *opus* should be *opuses*. There is no hope for such people.

[3] Some people want to blame Vincenzo Galilei and his Camerata gang, but they were just accessories before the fact.

[4] An oratorio is like an opera without scenery, costumes or action. It's much cheaper to produce but not half as much fun.

[5] The medical term for this operation is "bilateral orchidectomy." Now you know.

most of his contemporaries, both male and female.[6] He became a court singer for Philip V, the King of Spain. Every night, Farinelli would sing him to sleep. The King liked it better than a bedtime story.

The popularity of *opera buffa* grew out of short, comic plays with music, called *intermezzi*, written to be performed between the acts of the longer, more serious operas.[7] Among the most popular of these was one by Giovanni Battista Pergolesi, called *La serva padrona*. No self-respecting history of opera (of which this book is surely one) would be complete without a mention of this piece.[8]

Meanwhile, in France, Jean-Baptiste Lully had been combining music drama and ballet to form a French version of opera in such works as *Alceste* and *Bellerophon*. His promising career came to an abrupt end in 1687, when he died of a stubbed toe. It was Lully's practice to beat time on the floor with a heavy staff. You can see it coming: one day, in the middle of conducting a *Te Deum* for the king, he bashed his toe so severely that he developed gangrene and died.[9]

England never really got going on establishing its own form of opera, although Henry Purcell managed it once with *Dido and Aeneas*. The English were quite content to import Italian opera directly, or to let Anglicized outsiders such as Handel do it for them.[10]

The only uniquely English contribution to the development of opera is the masque, a poetical drama with music accompaniment. Thomas Arnes's masque *Alfred*, written in 1741, contains the song we now know as *Rule, Britannia*. Another English variant, known as the ballad opera, is really only a collection of popular melodies stolen from other operas and set to new words. John Gay's *The Beggar's Opera* is the most famous example. Copyright laws were much more slack in the 18th century, so although many people threat-

---

[6] Probably since he had nothing better to do with his spare time than to practise.
[7] Audiences back then had longer attention spans.
[8] Aren't I clever to have worked it into the narrative? Thank you.
[9] It was actually the blood poisoning that finally did it.
[10] For more on Handel's operas, please read the chapter on him earlier in this book. I don't want to go over it again.

ened him, Gay never lost any money over lawsuits.[11]

Big changes were in the wind with the arrival of a new German composer, Christoph Willibald Gluck, who decided that the long-established tradition of Italian opera made a mockery of the true intent of the dramatic plot. The *da capo* aria, with its built-in repeat, and excessive cadenzas inserted to allow the singers to show off, made Gluck very angry.[12]

A true opera fanatic.

His first big success was a new version of the old Greek myth first set by Monteverdi. Gluck's *Orfeo ed Euridice* was first performed in 1762, followed by *Alceste* in 1767. Another big triumph came with the Paris production in 1774 of *Iphigenie en Aulide*. This brought to an end a longstanding quarrel then raging in Paris between those who favored the French *opera comique* and others who favored the Italian *opera buffa*, which came to be called "The War of the Buffonists."

The Buffonists' rivalry was only one of the many that have

---

[11] Fittingly, one song from *The Beggar's Opera*, *Mack the Knife*, has become a standard of modern jazz singers, for which Gay gets no royalties. Serves him right.

[12] A petition presented to the Paris Opera management by a group of Italian singers demands that a cadenza must last "seven minutes and thirty-six seconds, all without drawing breath."

made the study of opera history so entertaining. Handel thought that Gluck knew no more about music than his cook, and the poet Franz Grillparzer once said of Carl Maria von Weber's opera *Die Freischütz*: "This opera can please only fools or idiots or pundits or street robbers or assassins."[13] But among the most famous is the disaster that accompanied the premiere performance of Gioacchino Rossini's opera *Il Barbiere di Siviglia* (*The Barber of Seville*).

Rossini composed his *Barber* in 1816 in little more than two weeks. Since time was short, he borrowed the plot of a story that had earlier been used in an opera by Giovanni Paisiello.[14] Paisiello was, not surprisingly, rather angry, so he sent a group of loyal friends to disrupt the opening night. They booed and hissed and threw things on the stage. This sort of distraction tends to upset the singers. One of them tripped on his robe; another broke a guitar string; and a third fell through the trapdoor. Then someone let a cat loose on the stage. The opera ended up being even funnier than Rossini had intended. The second night went much better: not a cat in sight. After that, Paisiello didn't have a chance.

Rossini was one of the most popular Italian opera composers of his day, so much so that he retired at 37 and devoted the rest of his long life (he died in 1868 at the age of 76) to becoming a gourmet cook and *bon vivant*. He grew quite fat, but he didn't care.

Rossini was a prolific composer and a very fast one who worked best under pressure. He wrote the overture to *The Thieving Magpie* on the day of the premiere in 1817. The impresario locked him in an upstairs room with four hefty bodyguards, who stood over him as he composed. As soon as he finished a page, one of the bodyguards would throw it out the window to a copyist waiting below. They were under orders to throw out Rossini if he didn't finish in time. His last opera was *Guillaume Tell*, written in 1829.[15]

---

[13] See yourself in there?

[14] Rossini borrowed some of the music, too. But mostly he stole it from his own earlier works, so that was all right. He had plenty to choose from: between 1810 and 1824 he composed 32 operas.

[15] A true opera fanatic is someone who can listen to the whole *William Tell* overture and never once think of *The Lone Ranger*.

There were lots of other Italian opera composers. Donizetti is all right, I suppose, if you like mad scenes. But the next really important composer is Giuseppe Verdi.[16] The respected music historian Donald Jay Grout makes a definitive summary of Verdi's contribution to music when he states: "Verdi is the only eminent composer in history who was also a successful farmer."[17]

When he wasn't out tending the crops, Verdi found the time to write 26 operas, including such favorites as *La Traviata* and *Aida*. He could have learned a thing or two from Rossini: he was asked to compose *Aida* for a celebration marking the opening of the Suez Canal in 1869. He didn't quite make the deadline.[18]

He did have this in common with Rossini: the opening night of *La Traviata* in 1853 was a disaster. The audience was shocked to see an opera performed in modern dress; the tenor had a bad cold and could hardly sing; and the audience couldn't stop laughing at the sight of the enormous leading soprano, who was supposed to be wasting away from consumption.[19]

There's more to be said about opera than I have space left for.[20] And I haven't even got to Bellini or Puccini or any of the other -inis, not to mention Hector Berlioz, Richard Strauss or any of the modern opera composers, such as Alban Berg or Igor Stravinsky.[21] My favorite of all the modern operas is *The Deliverance of Theseus*, written by the French composer Darius Milhaud in 1928. It's about seven minutes long. With a 10-minute intermission, I can just make it.

---

[16] At least that's what his father called him. The name on his birth certificate is Joseph Fortuninus Franciscus Verdi. He had a sister whom his father, in a flash of originality, named Giuseppa.

[17] I'm not sure what he farmed, but whatever it was he was good at it.

[18] What he needed was someone threatening to throw him out the window.

[19] There is a long tradition of overweight opera singers: Marietta Alboni, a favorite in Rossini operas, grew so huge that she could no longer move about the stage. She continued with a concert career, singing while seated in a big chair.

[20] See the earlier chapter on Wagner, for instance.

[21] A gas company in Breslau filed an injunction against Paul Hindemith's opera *Neues vom Tage* because the heroine sings a song praising electric heat over gas heat. The company felt it was bad for business.

THE MESS WE'RE
IN NOW

STRAVINSKY

STRAVINSKY MADE A BIG SPLASH when he started but became less and less controversial as he grew older. Maybe we just got used to him.

Igor Stravinsky was born in 1882 and grew up in St. Petersburg, where his father was an opera singer. His earliest memory as a child, he says, was the rhythmic sound of a peculiar clicking made by an old Russian peasant.[1] He began taking piano lessons in harmony and counterpoint.[2]

He studied law at St. Petersburg University, more to please his parents than any other reason. What he really wanted was to be a composer. He showed some of his early compositions to Rimsky-Korsakov, who became his teacher.[3] When Rimsky-Korsakov died in 1908, Stravinsky composed a funeral piece for him. Someone misplaced it during the Russian revolution.

Stravinsky's big successes came early in life, with the music that he composed for Serge Diaghilev and the Russian Ballet. The first of these was *The Firebird*, but the real surprise came with the next one, *Petrushka*, which the audience greeted with boos and hisses.[4]

The first performance in 1913 of *The Rite of Spring* became one of the greatest scandals in music history. More boos and hisses from the audience. Soon, fights broke out and there was as much mayhem in the seats as there was on stage. Stravinsky was lucky to get out of there alive. He said afterwards that the commotion wasn't because of his music at all, but resulted from "a gesture, too audacious and too intimate, which Nijinsky

---

[1] It was probably loose dentures.
[2] He found the harmony boring, but he liked the counterpoint.
[3] The older composer tactfully advised Stravinsky to continue his law studies.
[4] Stravinsky couldn't understand it: the dress rehearsal had gone so well.

made, doubtless thinking that anything was permissible with an erotic subject." There's no need to give credit to the dancer. Stravinsky was just being modest.

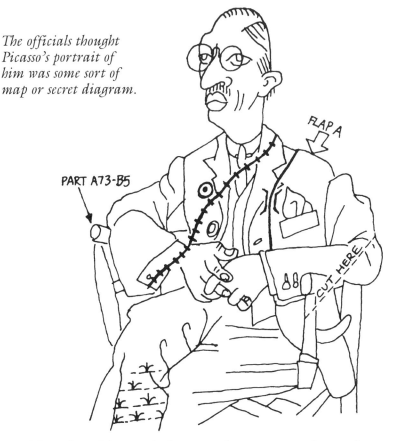

The officials thought Picasso's portrait of him was some sort of map or secret diagram.

After that, his music became less provocative as he moved into his "neo-Classic" style and later dabbled with serialism.[5] He also wrote odd little pieces here and there, including a jazzy clarinet concerto for the Woody Herman orchestra and a little dance for the Ringling Brothers circus.

The first performance was billed as "Fifty Elephants and Fifty Beautiful Girls in an Original Choreographic Tour de Force." It is safe to say that Stravinsky is the only composer in the history of music ever to write a polka for a troupe of elephants.[6] This was no joke: it was choreographed by George

[5] Dabbling with serialism is dangerous, like playing with dynamite.
[6] Jean-Baptiste Lully composed a *Concerto for the King's Bedchamber*, but it's not the same somehow.

Balanchine.[7] Stravinsky never saw the ballet, but he later met Bessie, the principal pachyderm, and shook her foot.[8]

Critics over the years have been rather unkind to Stravinsky. Writing about a piece Stravinsky composed in memory of Debussy, critic Ernest Newman said: "I had no idea Stravinsky disliked Debussy so much as this. If my own memories of a friend were as painful as Stravinsky's of Debussy seem to be, I would try to forget him." Another critic called one piece "a triumph of musical vacuity over the literary vigor of its text. ... The most invigorating sound I heard was a restive neighbor winding his watch."[9]

Stravinsky eventually moved to California and became an American citizen. The Boston police once wanted to fine him $100 for writing an arrangement of *The Star-Spangled Banner*.[10]

He often composed music on whatever paper was handy: napkins, envelopes or restaurant menus.[11] He liked to wear a battered, old green beret while he slept and once compared his music to his own nose:

"One does not criticize anybody or anything that is functioning," he said. "A nose is not manufactured; a nose just is. Thus, too, my art."

Well, that's one way of looking at it.

---

[7] Although the sight of 50 elephants in pink tutus must have been pretty funny.

[8] The elephant is the only animal that can be taught to stand on its head. It's also the only one with four knees, yet it cannot jump.

[9] Stravinsky got abuse from all sides. When Pablo Picasso painted his portrait, he had trouble crossing the border because the officials thought it was some sort of map or secret diagram.

[10] That's what he got for trying to be patriotic.

[11] Taking him to dinner could be hard on the nerves.

SCHOENBERG

W E REALLY SHOULDN'T BLAME Schoenberg. The way he tells it, at least, it wasn't his fault: "I am the slave of an internal power stronger than my education," he once said.

Elsewhere he said: "I am but the loudspeaker of an idea. The idea is an electric current — in the air. It may come from Jupiter — from the cosmos — that is not proven!"

The loudspeaker of an idea.

Arnold Schoenberg was not always a human radio receiver for musical broadcasts from Jupiter. By all accounts, his childhood was quite normal.[1] As an adult he was short, balding, and had large, bulging eyes. Maybe he read too much.

---

[1] The widow of Alban Berg, one of Schoenberg's pupils, claimed that Berg regularly talked with her from beyond the grave, giving instructions about his opera *Lulu*. It takes all kinds.

Schoenberg was born in Vienna in 1874 and began taking violin lessons at school when he was eight. After leaving school, he worked in a bank for a short time but that didn't work out. He began composing on his own, without instruction. Aside from a brief period when he took lessons in counterpoint from Alexander von Zemlinsky, Schoenberg remained almost entirely self-taught.[2] He married Zemlinsky's sister Mathilde, so the lessons were useful in more ways than one.

As a young man, Schoenberg took to hanging around the cafés in Vienna, drinking espresso and discussing the music of Wagner with all the other intellectuals who met there. He occasionally took jobs orchestrating music for the local operetta house. He didn't particularly enjoy the work, but he needed the money.

Schoenberg, by the way, usually spelt his name Schönberg, with the two little dots over the 'o,' which in German is called an *umlaut*.[3] If you leave out the *umlaut* you have to put in an extra 'e' to make up for it. Now you know.

Schoenberg never worried about how to spell his own name. He was too busy thinking about how to revolutionize the language of music. He started off simply enough, writing in a sophisticated, ultra-chromatic style that grew out of the works of Mahler.

But he went further than that, stretching the very limits of tonality to beyond breaking point. When the smoke had cleared, the structures of tonality that were the result of centuries of development lay in splinters on the floor, with Schoenberg standing in the wreckage. It was not a pretty sight.[4]

The system of composition developed by Schoenberg and later carried on by his pupils Berg and Anton von Webern came to be called serialism, or dodecaphony.[5] In it, the 12 tones that make up all the notes in an octave are arranged in a series, called a tone-row, from which all the melodic material for a piece of music is developed. Beyond that it gets too esoteric to explain.[6]

[2] Maybe that explains a lot.
[3] In English the proper name for those two little dots is diaeresis. But hardly anyone knows that.
[4] About as pretty as the mixed metaphors crashing around in that last paragraph.
[5] And a lot of other names that I'm too polite to mention.
[6] Schoenberg complained all through his life that no one understood him. It doesn't surprise me.

From the very beginning, Schoenberg's music was greeted with derision and disapproval by concertgoers. At the premiere performance of his first set of songs in 1900, there was a fist-fight in the audience. At the first performance of his *Chamber Symphony*, many people in the audience left early and made a lot of noise on the way out. They banged their fists on the seats, whistled loudly and jeered.

For his next recital, Schoenberg had a card printed up telling the audience that the purchase of a ticket entitled them to sit quietly and listen, but not to express their opinion of the music. It didn't do much good. When the fight during another performance led to a court case, a doctor testified for the defence that many in the audience had showed definite signs of neurosis as a result of listening to the music.

December 26, 1934 was an important day: in the *Suite for Strings in G major*, Schoenberg wrote his first proper key signature in 27 years just to show that he hadn't forgotten what they were for.

Schoenberg took up painting as a hobby for a while, and as a young man experimented with the concept of a typewriter for musical notation. Other than that, there wasn't much that could distract him from his self-proclaimed mission of "the emancipation of the dissonance."

He took this mission quite seriously: "It is my historic duty," he said, "to write what my destiny orders me to write."

Well, a man's gotta do what a man's gotta do.

THE ENGLISH
COUNTRY GARDENERS

RALPH VAUGHAN WILLIAMS was sitting around one morning, not doing much in particular, when he decided it might be fun to revive English music, which hadn't been doing very well lately.

Here it was 1903, and ever since the death of Purcell back in 1695 the fate of the English composer had been looking rather bleak.[1] Oh you can mention a few names — Wesley, Walmisley and crowd — but they spent most of their time hanging around the cathedrals.[2] You might also try to impress me with Delius and Elgar, but I'd know you were only bluffing.

Searching for English folk songs and ballads.

Vaughan Williams decided that the best way to go about doing this was to re-discover English folk songs. This meant tramping for hours across moors and walking about in a fen country. He and

---

[1] Especially for Purcell. He was never quite the same after he died.
[2] And you know what *that* means.

Gustav Holst used to do this for days on end, picking up folk songs, ballads, and country melodies, which they found lying around on the forest floor and scattered on village greens.

Eventually, Vaughan Williams collected about 800 of these tunes. Since it seemed a shame to see them go to waste, he often used them in his own compositions, to add a certain rustic appeal. Sometimes he made up little tunes of his own that sounded as if they should be folk songs. This was a little game he liked to play, just to keep in practice. As one biographer puts it, "he soaked himself in its melodic shapes and peculiar rhythms."[3]

Vaughan Williams was born in 1872 in Gloucester, but grew up in Surrey. His family was comfortably well off, which made supporting himself as a composer that much easier.[4] On his father's side was a long line of lawyers, although his father himself was a vicar in the Church of England. His mother was the daughter of Josiah Wedgwood.[5] Since she was also the niece of Charles Darwin, the evolutionist, and married to a church minister, I can only imagine what their dinner-table conversation was about.[6]

One of the big problems with Vaughan Williams is knowing what to call him. His great-grandfather had the simple last name of Williams; the "Vaughan" part seems to have crept in somewhere along the line. But everyone now calls the composer Vaughan Williams, and I'm not about to buck a trend. Then there's the problem of his first name, which looks like Ralph but probably ought to be pronounced "Rafe."[7]

Whatever his name was, he had a precocious musical talent. He composed his first piece at age six, a little four-bar piano tune called *The Robin's Nest*. After that, there was no stopping him. He went on to compose choral music, solo songs, church anthems, folk song suites, nine symphonies,[8] and six operas. When he was 10 years old he had also written a puppet opera, called *The Galoshes of Happiness*.[9]

---

[3] It was a wet business altogether. You know how much it rains in England.
[4] I would recommend this approach to anyone interested in composing: be born rich.
[5] That's the same Wedgwood family with all the plates.
[6] I don't think that Uncle Charles was invited over for dinner very often.
[7] This is the nation, remember, that pronounces Gloucester "Gloster."
[8] There's that magic number again.
[9] Well, it *was* an early work.

Most composers like to start off with a brilliant flash and then relax as they grow older. Not Vaughan Williams: he did much of his best work at an age when most composers are busy polishing their dentures. He composed his ninth and last symphony when he was 86, just before he died in 1958. All that walking as a young man must have been good for his health — not to mention those particularly happy galoshes.

❦ ❦ ❦

Benjamin Britten wrote no music about galoshes, but he did include a part for Slung Mugs in his musical play *Noye's Fludde*.[10] Britten was born in 1913 and as a young man set out to gather up all the folk songs that Vaughan Williams had carelessly left still lying about. He picked them up, brushed them off, and set them to music. Then he felt better. He also wrote 13 operas, including *Peter Grimes*, which is about a fisherman, and *Albert Herring*, which has nothing to do with fish at all.[11]

Albert Herring *has nothing to do with fish.*

Britten has often been called "England's second Purcell."[12] By happy coincidence, Britten was born on November 22, the day honoring St. Cecilia as the patron saint of music. Purcell died on St. Cecilia's Eve, so Britten was born the very next day only 218 years later. Some people see great significance in this. After all, what's a mere 218 years?

Britten died in 1976, having become Lord Britten and the Grand Old Man of English music. The position is currently vacant. Only serious applicants need apply.

---

[10] Slung Mugs are mugs that are slung from a string. Any old mugs will do. Just go get some from your kitchen.
[11] There are fish in *Billy Budd*, too. It takes place at sea, which is sometimes how audiences feel after hearing it.
[12] Or words to that effect.

IVES

·····················

CHARLES IVES (1874-1954) is to music composition what Henry David Thoreau is to philosophy: a rugged individualist, independent and strong willed. He didn't much care what other people thought about his music. He just went on composing the way he wanted to.[1]

Of course, it helped that he wasn't trying to make a living as a composer. Ives spent most of his adult life as an insurance broker in New York.[2] He married a woman named Harmony Twichell and lived a happy, middle-class life. He only composed in the evening and on weekends. On Saturdays he sometimes went down to the local beer hall and played ragtime piano.

Ives got much of his independent spirit from his father, George Ives. Ives senior was a bandmaster, the youngest one in the Union army during the American Civil War. One day he stood out during a thunderstorm listening to the church bell next door and spent the rest of the night trying to find the sound on his piano. It wasn't there.

This led George to invent what he called his "quarter-tone machine," an apparatus involving 24 violin strings and a series of weights and pulleys. He would compose quarter-tone melodies on the machine and have his young son Charles sing them back to him. Ives says that his father later "gave that up except as a form of punishment."[3] Another of his favorite tricks was to have Charles sing a popular song — *Swanee River*, say — in one key while he played the accompaniment in another key. He said he wanted to stretch the boy's ears.

---

[1] If he didn't agree with your opinion he was likely to call you a "nice old lady" or "lily-eared" or worse.
[2] He was the first to suggest double-indemnity insurance.
[3] The neighbors were complaining about the noise.

Charles Ives went on to study at Yale University, where his music teacher was Horatio Parker, a well-known composer. Ives liked Parker, although compared to his own father, Parker was a conservative old fuddy-duddy. His school record shows that he was only an average student in subjects other than music.[4]

He wanted to stretch the boy's ears.

Ives enjoyed his time at Yale: he was the winning pitcher against the freshman baseball team and later made the Yale football team. He composed not only his own "serious" music but also marches for the college band and music for fraternity vaudeville shows. All told, he wrote five symphonies and several large orchestral works, two piano sonatas, about 200 songs and more, all of it pretty weird. I find it ironic that he married someone named Harmony.

As a composer, he was so far ahead of his time that even today most listeners can't understand what he was getting at. He summed up his philosophy quite nicely when he wrote: "My God, what has sound got to do with music?!"

[4]His worst mark was 45 per cent in French.

WHERE DO WE GO FROM HERE?

CAGE

JOHN CAGE WAS THE *ENFANT TERRIBLE* of *avant-garde* music. English terminology just doesn't describe him adequately.

What is there to say about Cage's music? In keeping with his own philosophical approach as a composer, I could very well say nothing at all. "I have nothing to say," he says cryptically, "and I am saying it and that is poetry." Are you following this?

Cage was born in 1912 in Los Angeles. He was always a talker. When he was 17 he won a public-speaking contest and a year later he delivered his high-school valedictory address. He dropped out of college after two years and wandered around Europe for three years after that. Returning to California, he supported himself with a variety of odd jobs, including work as a gardener and bookbinder.[1] He also gave lectures in modern art and music to California housewives. He studied with various teachers, including Arnold Schoenberg, who said Cage had no feeling for harmony.

Cage has been called "the apostle of indeterminacy in music" for his explorations in the field of aleatoric music, or music involving randomness and chance. As a composer, Cage has shown greater determination than most of his music. He began to use tossed coins, thrown dice and the Chinese *I Ching* to determine aspects of performance.[2] His 1951 composition *Imaginary Landscape No. 4* calls for 12 radios tuned to different stations, chosen by tossing a coin.[3]

[1] He and three other bookbinders formed a percussion quartet.
[2] This was not entirely new. Mozart wrote a set of waltzes involving dice. So did Haydn and C.P.E. Bach.
[3] An earlier piece, *Credo In Us*, for four percussionists and radio, helpfully advises the player to "avoid News programs during national or international emergencies."

Around 1940, Cage developed what he called the "prepared piano," a piano with all sorts of different objects on the strings, which change the sounds the piano makes. It took him a while to discover the best way to do this. First he tried a pie plate, but that kept moving around. Then he tried nails, but they kept falling down beneath the strings. Finally he found that bolts and screws worked best, although he also used other objects such as rubber weatherstripping and pieces of paper.[4] His first piece for prepared piano was a dance-music suite called *Bacchanale*.

Cage's "prepared piano."

One chief characteristic of Cage's music is his use of unorthodox instruments or combinations of instruments. His piece *Living Room Music* needs four players of rhythmic parts incorporating "any household or architectural elements," including books, magazines, the furniture, the walls — whatever.[5]

For his *Music for Carillon No. 1*, he punched random holes in a piece of paper, then placed it over a graph to determine the pitch of the bells to be rung. *Branches* calls for percussive vegetables (non-percussive ones won't do), including pod rattles

[4] Don't try this at home, kids.
[5] That sounds more like a party I went to once.

and amplified cactus spines.[6] *Inlets* uses four players blowing conch shells and, in the background, the sound of pine cones burning.[7]

Cage was an innovator of all sorts different areas. He was among the first to set up living space in a New York warehouse loft, now a very trendy thing to do. His apartment was featured in the June 1946 issue of *Junior Harper's Bazaar* magazine. He knew more than you or I do about mushrooms, and in 1962 founded the New York Mycological Society for himself and other mushroom lovers.[8] He once said that, if he could do it all over again, he'd rather be a botanist.

August 29, 1952 was a historic day for modern music: Cage's piece *4'33"* was given its first performance, by his friend David Tudor in Woodstock, N.Y. In this piece, first performed on piano although intended for any instrument or ensemble, the performer merely sits in silence for four minutes and 33 seconds.[9]

This demonstrates Cage's belief that, in matters of structure, the integration of silence as an essential element is the "only new idea since Beethoven." Silence can never be total, Cage said.[10] There are always sounds around us: wind, birds, traffic, our own breathing, or whatever.[11]

"The music I prefer, even to my own or anybody else's," Cage once said "is what we are hearing if we are just quiet."

Cage died in 1992, in New York. Maybe it was all that noise.

Let us therefore have about 4 1/2 minutes of silence while we contemplate Cage's contributions to the development of music.

---

[6] You had to be there.

[7] If you don't want to use real pine cones, Cage says you can use a pre-recorded tape of pine cones burning, available at better record stores everywhere.

[8] He was also an honorary member of a mushroom society in Czechoslovakia. In 1958 he won $6,000 for correctly answering mushroom questions on an Italian television quiz show.

[9] Hence the catchy title. Compare these others: *59 1/2"* for string player; *31'57.9864"* and *34'46.776"* for pianist; *26'1.499"* for string player; and *27'10.554"* for percussionist. In 1962 he wrote *4'33" No. 2*, also known as *0'0"*. There's nothing to it.

[10] Just ask someone with small children.

[11] Some people breathe more loudly than others.

CODA

THIS BRINGS US TO A CLOSE in our study of music history. There's more to be said and still lots going on, but we'll need the benefit of hindsight to give us the proper perspective. Ask me again in a hundred years.

The benefit of hindsight.

BACH, BEETHOVEN AND THE BOYS:
Music History As It Ought To Be Taught

Published in Canada by

SOUND AND VISION
359 Riverdale Avenue
Toronto, Canada M4J 1A4

First printing, July 1986
24 26 28 30 - printings - 29 27 25 23

Canadian Cataloguing in Publication Data

Barber, David W. (David William), 1958-
Bach, Beethoven and the Boys

ISBN 0-920151-10-8

1. Music - History - Anecdotes, facetiae, satire, etc.
2. Composers - Anecdotes, facetiae, satire, etc.
1. Donald, David C. 11. Title

ML65.B37 1986 780'.9 C86-093755-0

Typeset in Galliard

Printed and bound in Canada

Also written by David W. Barber and illustrated by Dave Donald:

A MUSICIAN'S DICTIONARY (1983)
ISBN 0-920151-03-5

WHEN THE FAT LADY SINGS (1990)
Opera History As It Ought To Be Taught
ISBN 0-920151-11-6

IF IT AIN'T BAROQUE (1992)
More Music History As It Ought To Be Taught
ISBN 0-920151-15-9

GETTING A HANDEL ON MESSIAH (1994)
ISBN 0-920151-17-5

TENORS, TANTRUMS AND TRILLS (1996)
An Opera Dictionary from Aida to Zzzz
ISBN 0-920151-19-1

Other music books from Sound And Vision:

LOVE LIVES OF THE GREAT COMPOSERS
from Gesualdo to Wagner
by Basil Howitt
ISBN 0-920151-18-3

THE MUSIC LOVER'S QUOTATION BOOK
A Lyrical Companion
by Kathleen Kimball Melonakos
ISBN 0-920151-14-0

I WANNA BE SEDATED
Pop Music in the Seventies
by Phil Dellio & Scott Woods
ISBN 0-920151-16-7

HOW TO STAY AWAKE
During Anybody's Second Movement
by David E. Walden
ISBN 0-920151-20-5

If you have any comments on this book or any other books we publish, please write to us at Sound And Vision, 359 Riverdale Avenue, Toronto M4J 1A4, Canada or E-mail us at musicbooks@soundandvision.com.